'Tell it like it Wasn't!'

(The Art of Military Communication)

by
Brian (Harry) Clacy
and
Terry Cavender

CHAPTER 1
Henry V and his Army
(Battle of Agincourt - 1415)

CHAPTER 2
Admiral Nelson and Captain Hardy
(Battle of Trafalgar - 1805)

CHAPTER 3
The Duke of Wellington and Napoleon Bonaparte
(Battle of Waterloo - 1815)

CHAPTER 4
Captain Bairnsfather and German Lieutenant
(Christmas Truce - 1914)

CHAPTER 5
Field Marshal Haig and Field Marshal French
(Ypres - 1915)

CHAPTER 6
Captain Chavasse and Private Ratcliffe
(The Somme - 1916)

CHAPTER 7
Baron Von Richthofen and Captain Arthur Roy Brown
(The Somme - 1918)

CHAPTER 8
The Queen Mother and Benito Mussolini
(Rome - 1938)

CHAPTER 9
Winston Churchill and Charles de Gaulle
(London – 1940)

CHAPTER 10
Adolf Hitler and Generalfeldmarschall Paulus
(Berlin/Stalingrad – 1943)

CHAPTER 11
Wing Commander Bader and General Adolf Galland
(Colditz - 1944)

CHAPTER 12
Lieutenant Colonel Frost and Major General Urquhart
(Arnhem 1944)

CHAPTER 13
Brigadier Mike Calvert and Sergeant Bill Clift
(Burma 1944)

CHAPTER 14
Colonel Paul Tibbets and Crew in the Enola Gay
(Hiroshima - 1945)

CHAPTER 15
Lieutenant Colonel Carne and Chinese Officer
(Korea - 1951)

CHAPTER 16
Warrant Officer Class 1 (Regimental Sergeant Major) Brittain
(Royal Military Academy, Sandhurst - 1954)

CHAPTER 17
Grand Admiral Donitz and Prison Commandant
(Spandau Prison, West Berlin – 1956)

CHAPTER 18
General Douglas MacArthur and Lieutenant William Calley
(United States of America – 1969)

CHAPTER 19
Sgt 'Nobby' Clarke and Submarine Officer Fabricio Coloccini
(South Georgia - 1982)

CHAPTER 20
Epilogue

Acknowledgements

Harry and Terry would like to thank Nicky Clacy and Maggie Cavender (our Trouble and Strife's) for their patience and understanding during the process of writing this book. Harry was constantly shouting for help from Nicky who was usually working in her workshop upstairs, "Nicky! This bloody computer is doing it again…Nicky…oh bloody hell it's getting worse, NICKY!!! Can you come and have a look at this God forsaken computer, it's not doing what I tell it to do". Within seconds Nicky would appear like an Information and Technology guardian angel, she'd correct Harry's simple problem in quick time and explain where he went wrong and what to do if it happened again, she would then go back upstairs and continue with her own work. She never uttered a word of complaint even when Harry whinged, "It's doing it again and I can't remember what you told me to do"!

Terry Cavender is slightly less inept at computer 'trickery' but he also had to ask Maggie for help on many occasions, Terry thinks that Maggie and Nicky were very understanding every time the two authors disappeared into Beverley for a working lunch at Panizzi's restaurant and bar, the reality is that they were probably more than grateful for a bit of peace and quiet. Thanks for all your help.

We have to give an acknowledgement to ELK Marketing Agency in Beverley who have produce yet another excellent book cover. Eric Hartley (an IT genius) designed the book cover using the superb cartoon of a Regimental Sergeant Major in the Coldstream Guards. The cartoon was drawn by Bob Darkin who is an ex Warrant Officer Class II who served in the RAMC during the First Gulf War. Eric and Bob both did a top job for us and we greatly appreciate their help and attention to detail.

Brian (Harry) Clacy and Terry Cavender

Preface

This book is primarily a work of fiction which contains a large amount of facts thrown into it, "WHY" one hears you cry?

Well, have you ever tried to recall a conversation you've had with someone? Maybe you had to make a statement to the Police and during that interview you tried to relate who said what and to whom, the chances are that you probably couldn't remember word for word what was said and everything that actually happened. The only way, realistically, to remember a conversation accurately is if it was recorded or captured on film, but these day's even recordings can be digitally altered and so we have to rely on eye witness accounts of the facts and hope that they don't lie or have an over-zealous imagination.

The human race has dominated this planet for thousands of years and during that time we've written and recorded billions of books and documents, some of which are supposedly evidence of what people have said and done in real-life situations, but are they correct and accurate? For instance, we will never know exactly what the 1st Duke of Wellington said to Generalfeldmarschall Blucher after the Battle of Waterloo, but it has been recorded that the Iron Duke said,

"It has been a damned serious business Blucher and I have lost 30,000 men. It has been a damned nice thing and the nearest run thing you ever saw in your life by God! I don't think it would have done if I had not been there."

The above words were written long after the battlefield in Belgium was cleared of its casualties and the dead buried and we're not even sure if the great man even put the words down on paper himself. It's likely that the Duke sat down at his desk in Apsley House near Hyde Park in London, months after he'd returned to England, and probably started recounting the events of the famous battle to someone else. The words were probably changed time and again to make it more readable and glorious before the story was finally sent for publication.

So what is fact in all of the non-fiction books in our libraries and book stores? And we're not just talking about Wellington; was Joan of Arc really a Schizophrenic and what were her actual words when she took an English arrow through the shoulder during her Orleans campaign, surely it couldn't have been, "Lord, I suffer this pain in the pursuit of your glory." Our money is on her shouting, "Merde ca fait mal," translated into English that would be, "Shit, that stings!"

We can look at a couple of parables included in the Holy Bible to prove our point. Let us pray...I mean, let us take a look at the story about Noah and the

5

Ark. Incidentally, do you know what Noah's surname was? No... well neither do we, so for the purposes of this story Terry has re-christened him Noah Thistlethwaite who was allegedly born and raised in Keighley, West Yorkshire. God, Noah and Terry allegedly all come from the same town.

Genesis, Chapter Six, speaks of the conditions before the flood that led to the decision by the Lord (not the dark one) to destroy the Earth. Noah was instructed by God to "make an Ark" and fill it with two of every sort of living thing (good luck keeping the lion's and antelopes apart), and to gather "all food that is eaten" for their provisions (what the hell do Goliath Beetles eat?). In Genesis 6:11-22 the chapter ends with Noah's Ark being loaded with two of every sort and fully provisioned, "according to all that God commanded him." Noah died 350 years after the Flood and was apparently 950 years old when he finally popped his sandals. The following conversation between God and Noah is just as likely to have happened as anything else that is in Genesis 6:11-22:

God: "Noah – for the last time, are you there lad? It is I, the Lord."

Noah: "Oh no, it's that voice again. I'm going to have to ease up on this home brew."

God: "Noah, tha's going to have to talk to me afore ower long. I'm not giving in."

Noah: "All reyt, who is this?"

God: "I've just told thi, cloth ears – it's the Lord."

Noah: "What, as in the Lord God?"

God: "Yes! Give the man a gold star – he's finally latched on."

Noah: "Am I in bother for summat then?"

God: "No – I've got a task for thi."

Noah: "Oh, a task. There's allus a bloody catch with those task things. Go on then, what is it Lord?"

God: "I want you to build me an Ark."

Noah: "Absolutely no problem, Lord. Er, what's a bloody Ark?"

God: "Well, to cut a long story short, it's a humongous boat. It'll have to be big enough to take aboard two of every living things on earth."

Noah: "Are thee pulling me leg, me Lord?"

God: "No."

Noah: "Lord, does tha realise just how big a boat like that would need to be? I mean two elephants alone would fill it up! And what about those Giraffe's, have you seen how bloody tall they are?"

God: "You can do it Noah. I have every faith in you."

Noah: "Tha's definitely pulling me leg! I mean, summat that size, we're talking a lot of cubits there tha knows!"

God: "What's a cubit, Noah?"

Noah: "It's a unit of length based on the length of the forearm, from the elbow to the tip of the middle finger. There's some bloke down at our local DIY Store talking about some new-fangled measurement called feet and inches, but it'll never catch on."

God: "Well, you'll have to get cracking lad, t'storm clouds are gathering."

Noah: "Hell fire, I don't get a minute's peace. Incidentally, Lord, where am I going to get the brass to buy all the wood and nails and t'other bits and bobs, eh? And how am I going to feed everything eh? People and animals! I can't just nip into Morrison's now can I! Hell fire, the lads down at the Herod Arms'll never believe this!"

God: "I will provide. Tha mun have a bit of faith, cocker!"

Noah: "And what about a crew, where am I going to get them from? They don't just fall off trees, not that there's going to be any trees left if I'm going to build this blooming great Ark that tha's on about!"

God: "Tha mun take thi family with you as crew."

Noah: "Me family, they're bloody useless! They're allus fratching!"

God: "I've told you, Noah, you must have faith, lad!"

7

Noah: "Fair enough, I'll have a crack at this but I'm not having Faith! She's now't but trouble is that lass! Our Japreth's been sniffing round her for months. She's got a hell of a reputation!"

God: "Not that sort of faith, Noah."

Noah: "Don't lose heart, Lord. I'm starting to warm to this Ark lark. When does tha want me to get cracking? I can't do owt this weekend. We've got a feast coming up and t'wife's got to get some baking done."

God: "I'd advise you to crack on with the Ark as soon as you can, son. The storm clouds are looming."

Noah: "Fair enough Lord. I'll just finish this crate of home brew off then I'll go and speak to the lads and get summat fettled."

God: "You need to get a head of steam on. I'm not hanging on for too long."

Noah: "Fear not, Lord – leave it to Noah Thistlethwaite – my word is my bond. There's not a man in Keighley who wouldn't trust me."

God: "Fair enough. I'll give you a shout this time next week, see how things are going on like."

Noah: "Reyt. TTFN then, Lord."

God: "Er, TTFN Noah."

Is the above tête-à-tête any less likely than the things already written about what may or may not have happened before God allegedly flooded the entire world?

And what about the story of Joseph and Mary arriving at Bethlehem on Christmas Eve then? Let's look at what we think we know about this implausible fable. Joseph and his wife Mary entered the town of Bethlehem on the evening of 24th December in a year that was yet to be designated. Mary was heavily pregnant and her long journey riding on the back of a donkey would definitely have accelerated her labour pains. The pair of them were travelling from Nazareth to Bethlehem because, and I quote, **'he was of the house and lineage of David'** (God only knows what that means). Anyway, Joseph spotted an Inn on the edge of town and he halted the donkey outside the front door. It sounded like a party was in full swing and so he aggressively banged on the front door in the hope of getting someone's attention. Rather than the stuff written in the 'Good Book' we think the following conversation is just as likely to have taken place:

Joseph: "Hello! Is anybody there?"

Innkeeper: "Alright! Alright! Stop banging on the bloody door will you. You'll damage the woodwork! What do you want?"

Joseph: "Hi, we've just arrived in town and need somewhere to stay, have you got any spare rooms available?"

Innkeeper: "You're having a laugh aren't you mate, it's bleedin' Christmas Eve tonight! I've got a Shepherds' convention staying here for the week and they're a right bunch of pissheads. I've also got thirty shop stewards from the Carpenters Union arriving tomorrow. Every room's full old son, I'm sorry but you should have booked ahead."

Joseph: "We have travelled far and are in need of shelter and sustenance, can you not take pity on two poor travellers?"

Innkeeper: "Here, you're not from Galilee are you?"

Joseph: "No! We've tabbed it all the way here from Nazareth."

Innkeeper: "Good! Because I never have Fishermen in my gaff, they really stink the place up."

Joseph: "Can you help us in any way kind sir? My wife is heavy with child and I think she will give birth very soon."

Innkeeper: "You lot from Nazareth just can't keep it in your robes can you?"

Joseph: "No no! My wife is a virgin and she bears the new Messiah. The Arch Angel Gabriel visited her one night and decreed that God had chosen her to be the mother of his son."

Innkeeper: "I don't 'Adam and Eve' it, don't tell me that you fell for that old chestnut did you?"

Joseph: "But it is true, my wife swore unto me."

Innkeeper: "Hmmmm, my wife swears unto me as well but that don't mean she's telling the truth. Anyway, it don't make any difference who got your missus up the duff mate, there ain't no room at the Inn."

As Joseph turned to walk away Mary started to groan in pain on the back of the donkey and the Innkeeper called him back.

Innkeeper: "Listen, I've always been a sucker for a sob story. I really don't have any rooms available but there's a stable round the back of the Inn. You can kip in there for twenty shekels a night, it'll be self-catering though."

Joseph: "Oh kind Innkeeper how shall we ever be able to repay you?"

Innkeeper: "Well you can cough up the twenty shekels for starters."

Joseph started counting out the money from the pouch on his waist.

Innkeeper: "So, how far have you travelled to get here tonight?"

Joseph: "It cannot be less than eighty miles, kind sir."

Innkeeper: "Eighty miles! You've dragged that poor cow through the desert for eighty bleedin' miles, and on the back of a manky old donkey. Well I've never heard of anything so irresponsible! You should be bloody ashamed of yourself man."

Joseph: "But we are of the house and lineage of David."

Innkeeper: "So What!!!! Jesus Christ, you're a moron!"

Joseph: "Hey, Innkeeper, I like the sound of that. Mary, hear that?! What do you think of the name Jesus for the baby?"

We aren't being blasphemous, well maybe a little bit, but what we want to do in this book is look at similar 'real' points in history that have been recorded but remain slightly questionable. We're going to look at certain 'military' situations as we know them and put a more realistic bent on the partaker's conversations. This book takes the reports as we know them and then puts words into the mouths of historical military people to tell another less likely, but slightly plausible version of their unrecorded discussions during famous battles.

Before we get going, let's take a brief look at the Battle of Arnhem in 1944, aficionados of the film 'A Bridge Too Far' will probably recognise these lines from the movie. Picture the scene; after days of trying to make contact with 1st Airborne Divisions Headquarters, a 2 Para Radio Operator working near Arnhem Bridge suddenly makes radio contact. He says:

Radio Operator: "Bloody hell – the radio's working, I'm through to HQ, where's the Colonel!"

Paratrooper: "Down below!"

Radio Operator: "Well get him! Get him now!"

Paratrooper: "Colonel Frost? 'Scuse me sir!"

Lieutenant Colonel Frost: "What is it man?"

Paratrooper: "Up top…you're needed up top sir!"

Lieutenant Colonel Frost: "Why, what's happening?"

Radio Operator: "It's Headquarters sir…spark's has got 'em on the radio."

Lieutenant Colonel Frost: "Right, coming!"

The above words probably aren't the exact same words as those spoken on Arnhem Bridge in August 1944, but unless you were there on the day and dodging the bullets you'd never know the difference. And even if you were at the Battle, the chances are you had too many things to worry about other than remembering, verbatim, who said what and to whom. What you are about to read are real-life stories about real-life combatants who fought in real-life conflicts, the dates, places, names and wars about the actual protagonists are true as far as we know, but we've had to put some words into their mouths because no one really knows, word for word, what was said in the heat of each battle. We only know what was written, after the event took place.

"From the very mouths of Henry V at Agincourt to Colonel Tibbets flying the Enola Gay B29 bomber over Hiroshima, the words in this book could very well be the words that were actually spoken. The chances are that the dialogue in this book isn't particularly accurate though, because it's all guesswork using our overzealous imaginations. But then again, maybe this stuff is far more accurate than some of the drivel that's already in print. You be the judge.

1. HENRY V AND HIS ARMY
(AGINCOURT - 1415)

The British nation has never been afraid of getting involved in a punch up but due to the incompetence of some of our so called civilian and military leaders, a lot of the wars we've been sucked into have been made much harder to fight than was necessary. The Battle of the Somme and Dunkirk are just two that spring to mind. But when the odds are stacked against the English, Scottish, Irish and Welsh, these four nations have nearly always fought together and usually prevailed over much larger and better equipped armies. In fact, we Brits tend to prefer being outnumbered and surrounded in order to display our best fighting qualities and never more so than at the Battle of Agincourt.

The Anglo-French connection has always been something of a fragmented love/hate affair. Throughout history we've either bowed at each other's feet or tried to tear lumps off each other. During Henry V's reign, the borders of France and England looked like they had been drawn up by Jackson Pollock; England occupied and owned parts of Calais, Normandy, Touraine, Anjou, Brittany, Flanders and Aquitaine, which really annoyed our French cousins but pleased us immensely. Imagine how the English would have felt if the French nation had invaded and moved into Kent, Sussex and parts of Cornwall! They'd be more than welcome to Birmingham, Glasgow and Croydon, but we'd want to keep the good seaside stuff for ourselves?

England and France were both behaving like two socialite women who had turned up at a party whilst wearing the same black dress. Pouting, sulking and eye scratching was the order of the day. Anyway, young Aitch Five set off to France to sort out the garlic, and gastropod munching Gaul's. He was going because of some unpaid bill/ransom that needed sorting out. On 13th August in the year of our Lord 1415, Aitch Five tipped up at Chef-en-Caux in the Seine estuary with just over 10,000 English and Welsh hoodlums. Aitch's yobbos laid siege to Harfleur castle, which had a garrison of about 400 knee trembling French soldiers. The French garrison withstood every attack and held out for about a month before capitulating, Shakespeare wrote the following famous words that were supposed to have been said by Aitch Five during the final attack:

"Once more unto the breach, dear friends, once more
Or close the wall up with our English dead."
I see you stand like greyhounds in the slips
Straining upon the start
The games afoot, follow your spirit, and upon the charge
Cry God for Harry, England and Saint George!"

Roughly translated into modern speak Henry was saying:

"Come on lads, you're playing well, so don't give up now.
Our back four need to block those City strikers.
You're all playing your socks off but I need you to give me 110%.
It's the second half so let's get stuck in and challenge for every ball.
Listen to that crowd outside shouting, "UNITED, UNITED, UNITED!"

After the French had surrendered, Aitch Five left a small garrison of his soldiers to tidy up the mess and do a bit of pointing work on the damaged brickwork, he then headed north to the English garrison at Calais. On the way, Aitch Five, being the clever little sausage that he was, found a lightly defended bridge at Bethencourt-sur Somme where his army safely crossed the River Somme. Unfortunately, on the other side of the river the French Army had been alerted to the fact that the English were on the rampage yet again and they tried to 'head them off at the pass.' Aitch Five cleverly evaded the French Army but his escape route to Calais was eventually blocked when he reached the small town of Agincourt. The official figures vary depending on whose side you're on but even the French have to admit our happy 'band of brothers' were outnumbered by roughly 5 to 1. It is widely believed that Aitch Five arrived at Agincourt with 8,000 men at arms, the French Army numbering not much less than 40,000. The English Army was outnumbered, suffering from dysentery and were generally ball bagged after their arduous yomp from Harfleur, it looked like they were onto a hiding to nothing. Aitch Five sent his team, sorry I mean soldiers, out to recce the forthcoming battleground and they reported back that the pitch, sorry I mean battlefield, was waterlogged and the game, sorry I mean battle, might have to be postponed.

At first light on the morning of 25th October 1415 Aitch Five was doing the rounds of his soldiers when he heard Westmoreland, one of his senior commanders, chatting to other officers:

Westmoreland: "O that we now had here but ten thousand of those men in England that do no work today."

Which roughly translates into:

Westmoreland: "Bugger me, have you seen how many French are out there? We could do with ten thousand of those lazy bastards that are on the dole back home!"

Aitch Five was unmoved by the threat of overwhelming forces and according to Shakespeare he rallied his bedraggled soldiers, inspiring them with the following speech,

Henry V:

"What's he that wishes so?
My cousin, Westmoreland? No, my fair cousin;
If we are mark'd to die, we are enow
To do our country loss; and if to live,
The fewer men, the greater share of honour.
God's will! I pray thee, wish not one man more.
By Jove, I am not covetous for gold,
Nor care I who doth feed upon my cost;
It yearns me not if men my garments wear;
Such outward things dwell not in my desires.
But if it be a sin to covet honour,
I am the most offending soul alive.
No, faith, my coz, wish not a man from England.
God's peace! I would not lose so great an honour
As one man more methinks would share from me
For the best hope I have. O, do not wish one more!"

Which roughly translated meant:

Aitch Five: "I ain't bovvered, we don't need anyone else! We'll 'ave 'em all wiv just the blokes in our firm."

He then went on:

"Rather proclaim it, Westmoreland, through my host,
That he which hath no stomach to this fight,
Let him depart; his passport shall be made,
And crowns for convoy put into his purse;
We would not die in that man's company
That fears his fellowship to die with us.
This day is call'd the feast of Crispian.

14

He that outlives this day, and comes safe home,
Will stand a tip-toe when this day is nam'd,
And rouse him at the name of Crispian.
He that shall live this day, and see old age,
Will yearly on the vigil feast his neighbours,
And say "To-morrow is Saint Crispian."
Then will he strip his sleeve and show his scars,
And say "These wounds I had on Crispian's day."
Old men forget; yet all shall be forgot,
But he'll remember, with advantages,
What feats he did that day. Then shall our names,
Familiar in his mouth as household words-
Harry the King, Bedford and Exeter,
Warwick and Talbot, Salisbury and Gloucester-
Be in their flowing cups freshly rememb'red.
This story shall the good man teach his son;
And Crispin Crispian shall ne'er go by,
From this day to the ending of the world,
But we in it shall be remembered-
We few, we happy few, we band of brothers;
For he to-day that sheds his blood with me
Shall be my brother; be he ne'er so vile,
This day shall gentle his condition;
And gentlemen in England now-a-bed
Shall think themselves accurs'd they were not here,
And hold their manhoods cheap whiles any speaks
That fought with us upon Saint Crispin's day."

Again, roughly translated this meant:

Aitch Five: "Any of you geezers Ooo wanna bottle it an do a runner can piss off nah an I'll even give yer the bus fare 'ome. Anyone Ooo stays though and cuts up ruff wiv me, and 'opefully don't get is ead kicked in, will always be me bruv. Let's face it lads, if we come ahrt of this top dogs no-one's goin to come on ahr manor and give uz aggro. Those nob 'eads at Stamford Bridge'll be sorry they never came on this rumble."

Again, official figures differ but it is generally agreed that the battle of Agincourt resulted in the death of about 10,000 French knights and foot soldiers. The majority of these deaths were due to the awesome fire-power of the English bowmen. Aitch Five lost between 520 and 1,000 men at arms during the battle. Even today both nations still have a healthy dislike and grudging respect for each other.

2. ADMIRAL NELSON AND CAPTAIN HARDY
(BATTLE OF TRAFALGAR – 1805)

There can't be a more famous sailor than Horatio Nelson, even Sir Francis Drake and Walter Raleigh would have to take a back seat to this outstanding Royal Navy seadog. He was born in 1758 and got his sea legs when he was only 12 years old whilst serving on a Royal Navy ship that was commanded by his Uncle. A life at sea obviously agreed with him because he was promoted to Captain at the relatively young age of 20 and given his own command. Nelson turned out to be an inspirational Captain and leader who had a superb understanding of naval strategy and tactics. In 1793 he was given command of HMS Agamemnon in which he set sail for the Mediterranean. He displayed a fearless attitude when confronting the French and Spanish navies and was always at the front of the fighting. He was instrumental in helping the Royal Navy capture Corsica in 1794.

Always being in the thick of action was obviously going to increase his chances of getting wounded and Horatio lost the sight in one eye at the Siege of Calvi in 1794. Contrary to popular belief Nelson was only blinded in his right eye but didn't lose the eye itself and he never actually wore an eye patch. It was during the Battle of Santa Cruz de Tenerife in 1797 that Nelson was injured again but this time in his right arm. He was furious that the first part of his battle plan had failed and so decided to lead the next phase personally. It was whilst Nelson was landing in his boat that the Spanish defenders bombarded the landing party with grape shot and musket fire, Nelson was hit in his right arm. Nelson's Step-son, Lieutenant Nesbit, showed a great presence of mind by removing his own neckerchief and applying a tourniquet to stop the heavy bleeding. Back on his ship the navy surgeon had to partially amputate Nelson's right arm which for the rest of his life was a constant reminder of his own, and the British Royal Navies, failure to win the battle. During the Battle of Copenhagen in 1797 Nelson showed his tactical brilliance and total disregard for authority; his commander at the time thought they were losing too many casualties and signalled Nelson to disengage from the enemy. Legend has it that when Nelson was informed of the signal he lifted a telescope to his blind eye and said, "I see no signal" and continued on to win the Battle.

It was after defeating the French at the Battle of the Nile in 1798 that Nelson docked in Naples and was a guest at the home of the elderly Sir William Hamilton and his beautiful young wife Emma. By this time Nelson had prematurely aged because of his battle injuries and the weight of his naval responsibilities, he'd also lost nearly all of his teeth. Nelson was nursed back to health by Sir William's wife Emma and the pair of them fell in love. Sir William turned a blind eye to the affair because of his admiration for Nelson. When his health was restored Nelson was recalled to England, which coincided with Sir William's relief of post. Nelson and the Hamilton's returned to England and lived together in a ménage a trois.

In 1805 the Franco-Spanish fleet eventually came out of port and Nelson's fleet engaged them at the Battle of Trafalgar, this battle is thought to be the greatest of all British naval victories. Prior to the battle Nelson famously sent a signal to his fleet that read, 'England expects that every man will do his duty.' Less well known is that Nelson chose the word 'confides' rather than 'expects' but it was replaced because the word confides required more flags to be used. As the time for battle was fast approaching and the signal needed to be raised quickly Nelson agreed to the change. During the battle a French sharpshooter on the French ship Redoubtable fired a shot at Nelson, fatally wounding him. The musket ball hit Nelson in the shoulder and then severed his spine and as a result of which he died three hours later. His body was brought back to England in a sealed cask of brandy where the entire nation mourned his death. He was given a state funeral.

Captain Thomas Hardy

Thomas Hardy fought alongside Nelson at the Battle of Cape St Vincent, the Battle of the Nile and the Battle of Copenhagen during the French Revolutionary Wars. He was eventually appointed to serve as Flag Captain to Admiral Lord Nelson on HMS Victory at the Battle of Trafalgar in October 1805. Before the battle, Captain Hardy pressed for Nelson to transfer to another ship which would keep him safe from the fighting, Nelson argumentatively refused. As HMS Victory engaged with the enemy ships it came under heavy fire and Nelson was injured as he paced the quarter-deck with Hardy. The

Sergeant Major of Marines and two Seamen gently carried the fatally wounded Admiral below deck and Dr William Beatty, one of HMS Victory's physicians, was summoned to attend him.

As he lay dying in the ships cockpit, Nelson famously asked of his friend Captain Hardy to kiss him, and he did so before going back to the battle above.

Nelson lived for three hours after being injured and knew that his injuries were fatal. When Captain Hardy returned to inform Nelson that, "The Battle is won my Lord," he knew the Admiral hadn't long to live and so kissed him again, but this time on the forehead.   There are several theories about what Nelson's last words were but Captain Hardy heard him request, "Take care of my dear Lady Hamilton, Hardy, take care of poor Lady Hamilton." Unfortunately no-one did look after her and she died in poverty in Calais.

So, what would the conversation between Nelson and Hardy have been like whilst they walked about on the quarter-deck before he received that fatal injury?

NELSON AND HARDY

Nelson: Hell's teeth, Hardy, I feel as if someone has just walked over my grave."

Hardy: "T'would be a little difficult, sir?"

Nelson: "How so?"

Hardy: "Why, we have both requested to be disposed of at sea!"

They laugh heartily.

Nelson: "That, my dear Hardy, is in the lap of the Gods!"

Hardy: "Today, my Lord, all will be well. I have a good feeling about it. I smell victory once more."

Nelson: "You know, in truth, I weary of all this fighting. I'd much rather be at home with Lady Hamilton, sharing a glass of wine in front of a blazing log fire."

Hardy: "Wouldn't we all, sir – not with Lady Hamilton I hasten to add!"

Nelson: "Hardy – you are a wag! It'll be the undoing of you, sir!"

Again, they laugh gaily as they stroll around the deck of the Victory, seemingly without a care in the world, shot and shell flying around them.

Nelson: "It is good for the morale of the ship's crews to see that we are meandering around without, seemingly, caring not a fig, is it not so?"

Hardy: Aye milord, it imbues them with confidence, although I do wish that you'd take my advice and change your uniform. Too many shiny baubles for my liking. Johnny Crapaud has many snipers secreted in the rigging of their scows."

Nelson: "A pox on them, Hardy! I will not, like our enemies, hide behind plain clothing. Tis unmanly. Why, what would our jolly Jack Tars think of that, eh!"

Hardy: "T'other day, at Dinner, I was conversing with our Captain of Marines. He informs me that some of our Guards officers wear red uniforms in the event that if they are wounded then the men cannot see any blood, which would be a cause of disquiet."

Nelson: "Makes sound sense I suppose."

Hardy: "He then said that French and Spanish officers wear brown trousers in case they meet up with the Royal Navy!"

They both laugh.

Nelson: "Ha Ha, a vulgar but fine jest, Hardy. Let us return to the poop deck."

Hardy: "Aye aye, sir."

The battle was by then in full flow and at one point, a splinter took the buckle from Hardy's shoe.

Hardy: "Bugger it. A pox on those scurvy bastards! I paid good money for these shoes! The buckles are solid silver!"

Nelson: "They can be replaced, Hardy. Thank the Lord that the splinter didn't take your foot with it! Why, when this is all over I'll buy you a pair of buckles myself!"

Hardy: "I will take you up on that, my Lord."

Nelson: "This is too warm work to last for long, Hardy. A tumbler of Holland's gin wouldn't go amiss."

Hardy: "Indeed sir, but I have a distinct feeling that the day will be ours and that perhaps some captured French champagne would slip down nicely."

Nelson: "Undoubtedly. Just look at how our men answer the enemy! I have every confidence in our brave lads and their officers. They, like you and I, will do their duty, of that I have no fear."

Hardy: "Aye sir, there are many honest men amongst their ranks. Makes me heart swell with pride."

There is the crack of shot and shell whistling by.

Nelson: "So much metal flying through the air today, Hardy. Like swarms of bees, is it not so?

Hardy: "Indeed. You know sir...   I say, is anything wrong sir?"

Nelson: "Dammit, I am hit, Hardy. Help get me below before it is noticed. Cover my wound with a handkerchief, quickly man, I feel my legs giving way."

Hardy: "You there! Give me hand with the Admiral! He has been winged."

Nelson: "Quickly Hardy, strangely, I feel that I do not have long."

Hardy: "Move yourselves, damn you – and be gentle with the Admiral there!"

Nelson: "Hardy, send for the Chaplain, if you will."

Hardy: "Oh my Lord, fear not, the Surgeon will soon resolve this issue. You'll be back on deck in no time."

Nelson: "I fear not Hardy, but thank God I have done my duty."

The Admiral is taken to the Surgeon.

Footnote. In September of 1805 a soldier and sailor were sitting opposite each other in the waiting room in Downing Street. They were both to be interviewed by the Secretary for War and the Colonies, after returning from India and the Caribbean respectively.   Although unknown to each other they started a conversation which the soldier later described as, "almost all on his side in a style so vain and silly as to surprise and almost disgust me."

As the sailor was missing his right arm the soldier quite rightly deduced that he was in fact Britain's greatest naval hero, Lord Nelson. The Admiral briefly left the waiting room to enquire from a clerical officer who the soldier was. When informed that the 'squaddie' was Arthur Wellesley, the Duke of Wellington, Nelson returned to the waiting room and they then continued their conversation as equals.

This was the only time the two men are believed to have met. Six weeks later Nelson was killed at the Battle of Trafalgar.

3. THE DUKE OF WELLINGTON AND NAPOLEON BONAPARTE (BATTLE OF WATERLOO – 1815)

The Duke of Wellington was a British Soldier and statesman and one of the leading military and political figures of the 19th century. Christened Arthur Wellesley he was commissioned as an ensign in the British Army in 1787 and was promoted to Full Colonel just nine years later. In 1803 Arthur saw action in India where as a newly promoted Major General he won a decisive battle over the Maratha Confederacy at the Battle of Assaye.

It was during the Napoleonic Wars that he really came to prominence and after defeating Napoleon's Army at the Battle of Vitoria in 1813, he was promoted to the ultimate rank of Field Marshal. Napoleon Bonaparte was put in exile in 1814 but to the victor the spoils must go and Arthur Wellesley was granted a Dukedom and made the Ambassador to France. During the Hundred Days War in 1815 the Duke commanded an Allied Army which, with a little bit of help from the Prussian Army commanded by Feldmarschall Blucher, he again defeated Napoleon Bonaparte, but this time at the Battle of Waterloo.

A little after two o'clock on the 18th June 1815, when Wellington had just finished lunch, Napoleon launched an attack on Hougomont Farm. This iconic battle ground was being heroically defended by Wellington's totally surrounded 3rd Regiment of Foot Guards (later the Coldstream Guards). Wellington ordered flanking attacks on Napoleon's Old Guard who were attacking down the centre, the farmhouse had to be saved at all costs. The cost was high, many men and horses died during the ferocious battle and it looked certain that Wellington was about to lose the campaign. General Feldmarschall Blucher and his Prussian Army turned up late for the 'party' but in the nick of time. They attacked and drove straight into the middle of the French Army and helped the British to devastate Napoleon's Old Guard. The battle was won by the British and Prussians because Napoleon had no other reserves to call upon. Wellington rushed down to the farm and waited for Blucher to arrive so that they could celebrate a victory that both Field Marshals' claimed as their own. Tradition in those days dictated that the victorious commanders had to agree on a name for the battlefield so they could reap any historical benefits. The debate was also won by Wellington who decreed the battle site should be known as Waterloo.

Although Arthur and Napoleon never actually met face to face, the following conversation could possibly have taken place had the two protagonists met on the battlefield at Waterloo at a small tavern, 'La Belle Alliance.'

Wellington: "Your Imperial Majesty, may I offer you some refreshment, a glass of wine mayhap?"

Bonaparte: "Only if it is French, your Grace!"

Wellington: "Come, come sir, we are civilised men, I would not insult your palate with anything less."

Bonaparte: "Very well, Field Marshal, that is most generous of you."

Wellington: "Not really, to be perfectly honest my fellows 'rescued' it from your royal baggage train, along with numerous other interesting items."

Bonaparte: "Merde - to the victor the spoils, eh!"

Wellington: "You should not be bitter sir, I'm sure you would have been delighted to gain possession of such items had the situation been reversed. I'm afraid that the 14th Light Dragoons collared your chamber pot!"

Bonaparte: "I will just have to make alternative arrangements for my ablutions! You know, your Grace, you had the luck of the devil! Had Blucher and his troops not appeared when they did and tipped the balance in your favour, then the victory would undoubtedly have been mine!"

Wellington: "Well they did – and you didn't! Fortunes of war, eh! Come along sir, drink up!"

Bonaparte: "It is so strange, here we are sharing a glass of wine together in front of a blazing log fire. We have been sworn enemies for so long and yet we have never crossed paths."

Wellington: "Or swords! Although I have espied you, astride your horse galloping around the battlefield."

Bonaparte: "Ah yes - that would be on my Desiree, a wonderful mount."

Wellington: "Yes, damned fine things horses. My 'Copenhagen' should have been a lion – he has the heart of one! Never flinches under fire."

Bonaparte: "Arthur, may I call you Arthur?"

Wellington: "An honour indeed. May I call you Napoleon?"

Bonaparte: "Be my guest. We are just two simple Warlords when all is said and done. Ha, do you know what our troops call us?"

Wellington: "It'll be something rude knowing those foul mouthed bastards!"

Bonaparte: "The Peacock and the Professional!"

Wellington: "Ah! But which one of us is which?"

Bonaparte: "Ha ha, it would, sir, be a brave man who would call you a Peacock to your face!"

Wellington: "I'll settle for 'Professional' then. Yes, that'll do for me. A splash more wine?"

Bonaparte: "Perhaps one more glass before I depart for St Helena."

Wellington: "Ah, going on extended leave are you? I should have a good rest if I were you. You deserve it after today's efforts"

Bonaparte: "So, banished once to Elbe and now it is to be St Helena. There will be no more battles for Napoleon Bonaparte, methinks. The French people are a puzzle within a puzzle! No doubt they will welcome that fat oaf Louis the XVIII back from where he is skulking."

Wellington: "Oh, never say die old chap. You know how quickly things can turn around."

Bonaparte: "Alas I am now in the unwelcome and inescapable arms of Perfidious Albion! I am finished. Napoleon Bonaparte is finished."

Wellington: "I say, steady on old chap. It was a well fought fight, but you were beaten fair and square. Someone has to win and someone has to lose, eh."

Bonaparte: "Yes, but defeat is a bitter pill for me to swallow. And you know, it is very difficult for history to get at the real facts. Luckily they are more often objects of curiosity than truly important. There are so many facts."

Wellington: "You know what this old military game is like as well as I do. One minute you're up there in the saddle waving your hat and sword, celebrating victory and the next you're flat on your arse in a pile of horse-shit, winded."

Bonaparte: "The worst of it is that I shall never be able return home to see my beautiful Josephine, or Paris, again."

Wellington: "Come, come now, Napoleon, don't get maudling. There's plenty of other fish in the sea for people like you and I. If I may, what about those other two women I've heard spoken of around the camp fires?

Bonaparte: "Other women, Monsieur?"

Wellington: "Well, er, Guiseppina Grassini and Marguerite-Josephine Weiner. Both delectable bits of crumpet, if you'll pardon my French!"

Unbeknown to Napoleon, Wellington had also enjoyed the company of these 'ladies' who often compared notes on their lovers; Wellington came out on top in this department as well.

Bonaparte: "Crumpet you say, what a quaint English phrase. Huh, you are well informed, sir?"

Wellington: "I must admit to having my ear well to the ground. There's nothing wrong with having a fair maiden or two on the side, eh! I'm a bit of a swordsman myself if truth be known. Come, finish your wine, there's a good little Emperor. I see that your coach has arrived."

Bonaparte: "I drink to your victory, Arthur Wellington. It is indeed historic."

Wellington: "Yes, well they're already saying that it's the greatest victory since Agincourt you know."

Bonaparte: "I'm sure that you will be amply rewarded by a grateful nation. Titles, medals, pensions, property. I, conversely, have lost everything."

Wellington: "Oh, don't be despondent old chap. I'm certain that we'll both be celebrated in our own way – in our own countries. History will not be unkind to either of us."

Bonaparte: "I must take my leave, your Grace, if you are ever passing St Helena, you have an open invitation to come and share a glass of wine, French of course, with me. It would be an honour to meet you again."

Wellington: "Indeed. I might just take you up on that."

Bonaparte: "Au Revoir, Arthur Wellesley."

Bonaparte takes his leave of Wellington.

Wellington: "ADC!"

ADC: "Your Grace?"

Wellington: "Get rid of this pissy French wine will you! Let's have a decent barrel of English ale brought in here – oh, and make sure that Boney is shown off the premises with due decorum as befits his station! Instruct those fucking soldiers of mine that if I hear just one raspberry, I'll have the man responsible flogged until the whites of his bones show! Do you hear!"

ADC: "Indeed your Grace. No raspberries!"

Wellington's battle record is exemplary. After participating in some 60 battles during the course of his military career, he is regarded as one of the greatest defensive commanders of all time. Wellington remained Commander-in-Chief of the British Army until his death in 1852.

4. CAPTAIN BAIRNSFATHER AT THECHRISTMAS TRUCE
(YPRES – 1914)

Captain Bairnsfather
(Photograph by Pirie MacDonald)

Young people today probably won't have a clue who Captain Bruce Bairnsfather was and yet during the First World War he was one of the most famous men alive. Bruce was born in 1887 in the British Army Garrison of Murree India (now a part of Pakistan). His father, Major Thomas Henry Bairnsfather, was an Officer serving in the British Army at the time. On completion of his posting to India the Major and his family returned to England where Bruce finished his education at Westward Ho! in Devon and latterly at Stratford-upon-Avon. Bruce had decided on a career in the British Army but the results of his entrance exams at Sandhurst and Woolwich military academies just weren't good enough. To compensate he enlisted into the Cheshire Regiment for a few years, resigning his commission in 1907 and studied art instead. The art world wasn't kind to him though, so he trained and qualified as an electrical engineer to provide himself with the means to live. Whilst working as an electrician in a Stratford theatre he was introduced to Thomas Lipton (of Lipton's Tea fame) and this chance meeting led him into being commissioned to draw some advertising sketches for various consumable products like Tea, Cigarettes, Mustard and Beecham's powders.

On the outbreak of the First World War, Bruce re-enlisted into the Army as a Second Lieutenant in the Royal Warwickshire Regiment. On Christmas Eve 1914 he became involved in one of the most incredible incidents ever experienced by soldiers at war. The Warwickshire Regiment went back into the line at Saint-Yves near Ploegsteert (pronounced Plugstreet by British Soldiers) near Ypres. It was a very cold and frosty 23rd of December and there was an absence of small arms fire and shelling by both sides, so all was bizarrely quiet on the Western Front. The following night, Bruce had been invited to another British dugout for a trench dinner where he sampled some red wine and tinned delicacies that had been sent from home. After dinner he made his way back to his own dugout where he found the men of his platoon cheerfully standing around the trench telling jokes and jibing with each other. One of his soldiers saw him arrive and said, "You can 'ear 'em quite plain sir!" "Hear what?" Bruce inquired. "It's them Germans over there sir, we can 'ear 'em singin' and playin' in a band or somethin." Guttural singing could be heard from the German trench opposite where they were performing, 'Deutschland, Deutschland, uber Alles' which was followed by 'Stille Nacht, Heilige Nacht' (Silent Night, Holy Night). The British replied with 'God Save the King,' followed by some popular ragtime songs which the Germans seemed to enjoy, so much so that they shouted, "Tommy! Why don't you come over and visit us, we won't shoot you." The British soldiers roared with laughter and a lot of banter was exchanged between both sides, but the German soldiers refused to allow the repartee to stop and again asked the British to come across. It took the courage, trust and initiative of a British Army Sergeant and a German soldier to break the deadlock though; the Sergeant went out into no man's land armed only with a couple of tins of Machonochie stew and some Capstan cigarettes. He met the German soldier in the middle of the trenches and they both chin-wagged for a couple of minutes before returning to their own lines, the German with his tins of stew and English cigarettes and the British Sergeant with a gift of German cigars.

In the morning, 2nd Lieutenant Bairnsfather ventured over the parapet and walked into the middle of no man's land where a couple of dozen German and British soldiers were fraternising with each other. Bruce observed, "Here were these sausage eating wretches, who had elected to start this infernal European fracas, and in doing so had brought us all into the same muddy pickle as themselves - I wouldn't have missed that unique and weird Christmas Day for anything." During the day the British and German soldiers shook hands and talked about the futility of trying to kill each other, they also buried their dead and exchanged gifts of food, alcohol, sweets and cigarettes. Legend has it that a football match was held between the German and British soldiers and that we lost 3-2, but with all the shell holes in no man's land this seems unlikely.

During the truce Bruce spotted one of his Machine Gunners (a barber in civilian life) cutting the long hair of a German soldier whilst they were both standing in no man's land. He also caught the eye a German Lieutenant and went over to have a chat with him. The two men exchanged a couple of buttons from their uniforms and carried on doing the social rounds as if they were in the ante room of the Officers' Mess. Photographs were taken of this inconceivable social gathering, during which Bruce used his drawing skills and sketched some images of the fraternisation. These weren't the only soldiers to take part in a Christmas truce either, socializing also went on in other parts of the front line between French and German soldiers but to a lesser degree, probably because the German Army had invaded French soil and their soldiers weren't quite as amenable as the British lads.

Within a year Captain Bairnsfather was suffering from hearing problems and 'Shell Shock' that he'd sustained during the Second Battle of Ypres. He was evacuated to England and on release from hospital was posted to a training unit based on Salisbury Plain. It was during this respite from the Western Front that Bruce started producing some humorous sketches of life in the trenches. The drawings were printed in the Bystander Magazine and became massively popular at home and abroad. One of his characters that became a firm favourite with the troops was 'Old Bill', a grumpy and cantankerous old soldier who had a walrus moustache and wore a trench balaclava. Some people believe that the nickname for the London Police derived from this character and his moustache. Arguably, his most famous sendup was of two British Tommy's sitting in a shell hole in no man's land with shells bursting all around them, one saying to the other, "Well, if you knows of a better 'ole, go to it."

No-one knows for sure exactly how the conversations between friend and foe took place that Christmas Day at Ploegsteert, but because of the differences in language it must have been difficult and probably went something like this:

Bairnsfather: "Good morning and how are you on this fine day old boy? Or should I say - Guten Morgen alt sohn."

German Lieutenant: "Alt Sohn????"

Bairnsfather: "Yes. You know…it's a term of endearment…if a cockerney in London likes you he will call you old son.. alt sohn…I like you…alt sohn!"

German Lieutenant: "Alt Sohn????"

Bairnsfather: "Crikey O'Riley Fritz! You're determined not to make this easy aren't you?"

German Lieutenant: "Mein name ist Maximilian."

Bairnsfather: "Oh I say…isn't that lovely…well done Max, such a good strong name…were you named after the machine-gun…oh no, perhaps we'd better not go down that road just now."

German Lieutenant: "Wie ist ihr name?"

Bairnsfather: "Oh yes...good question...what is my name? Well of course I know my name but it's just how I'm going to explain it to you old bo...no, better not start all that again."

German Lieutenant: "WIE IST IHR NAME?"

Bairnsfather: "Yes, just coming to it Max... well as it happens, mein name ist Captain – that's Kapitan Bruce Bairnsfather".

German Lieutenant: "Bairnsfather?"

Bairnsfather: "Well it's a bit like this, in the North of England and Scotland those indigenous people call their children bairns which is the first part of my name. The second part is father, which means daddy."

German Lieutenant: "Fahrter????"

Bairnsfather: "Yes, well it's the old Brussel sprouts he eats I suppose, anyway moving on, any chance of swapping a couple of buttons my good man?"

German Lieutenant: "KNOPF!"

Bairnsfather: "No need to be rude."

German Lieutenant: "Button ist knopf in Deutsch."

Bairnsfather: "Oh I say, isn't that just super, would you mind awfully if I had a look at one? What's that wording around the top?"

German Lieutenant: "GOTT MIT UNS, in English zis means zat God is viss us. He is on our side."

Bairnsfather: "Oh bless your cotton socks old boy! Do you actually believe that?"

German Lieutenant: "Jawhoul, Herr Kapitan!"

Bairnsfather: "Sorry for putting some Sauerkraut on your Lebkuchen, Max, but we have it on good faith that the big chap is on our side...you know Jerusalem...green and pleasant land...all that sort of stuff."

German Lieutenant: "NEIN!"

Bairnsfather: "No, it's nearer twelve actually, it'll soon be time for Tiffin, I think."

German Lieutenant: "You damned English alvays sink you are right."
Bairnsfather: "Yes well that's probably because we usually are. Anyway, got to go, so chin chin old chap. With a bit of luck the top brass will sort it all out and we can remain good friends eh?"

German Lieutenant: "Ja, but you vill lose zis var."

Bairnsfather: "Yes, well…, and I suppose you think the sun will also set on the British Empire as well. Let's face it, you think Germany will win this war and I think the British Empire will never collapse. At least one of us is laughing up his Schleiffenplan."

5. FIELD MARSHAL HAIG AND FIELD MARSHAL FRENCH
(YPRES - 1915)

Field Marshal Douglas Haig was, and remains a conundrum; there are three camps when it comes to this famous British Army officer. One, people love him, two, people hate him, and three, people really couldn't care less about him. He was a cavalry officer who entered the hallowed gates of the Royal Military Academy at Sandhurst in January 1884 and was commissioned as a Lieutenant in the 7th (Queens Own Hussars) on 7th February 1885. He ultimately commanded the British Army in France and Belgium for most of the First World War, rising to the rank of Field Marshal.

Those in the 'love him' camp will tell you he saw action in the Sudan and Boer Wars, those in the 'hate him' camp will tell you that a British Officer going up against a few natives armed with some blunt spears, whilst shooting them with modern bolt action rifles, does not count as seeing action. It must have been more like being present at a turkey shoot and watching it from the safety of the back row. Those in the 'couldn't care less' camp will say "Who cares."

During the Boer war, the then Major Haig was responsible for carrying out a British scorched earth policy, this included burning down farms, rounding up women and children, and imprisoning them in concentration camps where a lot of them died from starvation and disease (looks like the Germans weren't the first then). Those in the 'love him' camp will tell you that he was diligently carrying out his orders to the best of his abilities and that was how things were done in those days (the Germans could say the same thing I suppose). Those in the 'hate him' camp will tell you that Haig lacked any sort of compassion because he was a humourless and arrogant prig and that he was only interested in his own advancement in the British Army. Those in the 'couldn't care less' camp will say "So what, it all happened a long time ago?"

Haig had started playing polo for the British Army soon after receiving his commission at RMA Sandhurst and at matches he made important social connections which included the heads of the royal family. He made the most of these upper class get-togethers and generally ingratiated himself with anyone who could help enhance his military career. Those in the 'love him' camp will tell you that there is nothing wrong with trying to improve your station in life. Those in the 'hate him' camp will tell you he was a royal kiss arse, and those in the 'couldn't care less' camp will say "I really don't give a shit about him."

'Dougie' then took up the post of Inspector General of Cavalry in India before becoming Aide de Camp (a really posh kiss arse job) to King Edward VII for two years. As a result of that posting he was promoted to Major General in 1904, at that time being the youngest officer to have ever achieved that rank. Those in the 'love him' camp will firmly believe that he accomplished this through hard work and without, metaphorically, stabbing anyone in the back or kissing any bottoms. Those in the 'hate him' camp will say, "He must have got a really good shine on the King's riding boots." Those in the 'couldn't care less' camp will just shrug their shoulders and say "Have you seen the price of prunes?"

A few more years on and back in India as a Chief of Staff, good old Doug was promoted to Lieutenant General. He then got his boot brushes out again when he was appointed Aide de Camp to King George V in 1914 (he must have been very good at shining boots). It was during this period that Haig showed his true character when he started bitching to the King behind the backs of his senior officers. He told King George V that Field Marshal French wasn't good enough to lead the British Army in any likely future European War. Just before the start of World War One, Dougie took over as the General Officer Commanding of Aldershot Command; with two Divisions and a Cavalry Brigade under his command he must have been chuckling with glee. The smile was quickly wiped off his face though during some Army manoeuvres, despite all the odds and advantages being in Doug's favour, Sir James Grierson unequivocally thrashed him in the war game (apparently Sir James Grierson made better use of his Air Reconnaissance). Those in the 'love him' camp will say, "Grierson probably cheated" and those in the 'hate him' camp will say it was just a small indication of Doug's incompetence and a sign of things to come. Those in the 'couldn't care less' camp will say, "For goodness sake leave me out of this will you!"

On 4th August 1914 Britain declared war on Germany and Field Marshal French set off to France with his 1st and 2nd Corps to help the French Army slap the Kaiser and his Teutonic hooligans. Haig was in command 1st Corps and Lieutenant General Horace Smith-Dorrien (an Infantry trained officer) commanded 2nd Corps. Horace Smith-Dorrien distinguished himself during the battle of Mons and, against orders, engaged with the German Army to stop their headlong and determined onslaught. Whilst he was doing this, Haig was retreating at full pelt and left a massive gap between the two Corps that the Germans could have exploited. Haig also sent exaggerated reports to his boss,

Field Marshal Sir John French, at his Headquarters and this caused Sir John to go into a furious panic. Those in the 'love him' camp will say, "Horace Smith-Dorrien was an irresponsible renegade who got lucky and that Haig was just giving a full and accurate report. Those in the 'hate him' camp will say that "Haig got a twitchy bum, legged it and dropped his 'comrades' right in the shit." Those in the 'couldn't care less' camp will say, "What time is tea?"

The Kaiser's Army kept trying to do a right flanking movement round the British Army so that they could complete their Schlieffen Plan. They hoped to encircle Paris and force the French to surrender. The British Army urinated on their bonfire though because as the Germans tried to outflank them, the British Army kept re-outflanking the Germans. This resulted in what has become known as the 'Race to the Sea' which ended at Nieuwpoort in Belgium; and so started four years of trench warfare that stretched over a distance of four hundred miles. In 1915 Sir John French and the British Army suffered a dreadful defeat at the Battle of Loos. The Field Marshal was blamed and de-gummed, which in army speak meant removing him from his high profile position, he was put into a routine command back in Britain. Haig also stuck the knife into the Field Marshal's ribs by telling King George V that Sir John French was "a great source of weakness to the Army and that no-one had any confidence in him" (with friends like him…). When Haig was promoted to Field Marshal and given command of the entire British Expeditionary Force, the King sent a note to Haig informing him that his Field Marshal baton was a belated Christmas present. Those in the 'love him' camp will say, Haig did his country a service by exposing Sir John French as an inept and useless arse. Those in the 'hate him' camp will say that Haig was a treacherous, inept and useless arse. Those in the 'couldn't care less' camp will say, "They were all inept and useless arses."

Haig had dinner with King George V who was visiting France to find out what went wrong at the Battle of Loos. Good old Dougie told his Majesty that "French should have been sacked in August 1914." The following day the King went riding and was thrown from one of Haig's horses and much to Dougie's embarrassment his Majesty suffered a back injury resulting in the King having to be evacuated to England on a stretcher. The two Field Marshals did a final handover/takeover on 18th December 1915, their frosty meeting may well have been similar to this:

Douglas Haig: "Morning John."

John French: "That's <u>Sir</u> John to you, arse-wipe! I am still your superior officer until I hand over command!"

Douglas Haig: "Look, can't we at least keep this meeting adult and civilised?"

John French: "You don't know the meaning of the word civilised, you bounder! At every turn you have distrusted our French allies and have caused dissent about my orders and plans with the War Office."

Douglas Haig: "The French cannot be trusted and for that very reason I feel the British Army should operate independently of them. Look at that old French fool Joffre at Mons, he withdrew the French army all the way back to the Marne and we had to do the same."

John French: "As I remember, you were pretty quick off the mark when Fritz and his mates started coming over the hill, I don't like the cocky little sod but you left Horace Smith Dorian to face the brunt of the German Army on his own."

Douglas Haig: "He defied your orders…if you recall?"

John French: "Don't care, he saved your arse…if you recall."

Douglas Haig: "Ner, neh ner."

John French: "So much for keeping this adult and civilised".

Douglas Haig: "Can we just get on with the handover/takeover please? I think you are behaving like a self-obsessed tyrant."

John French: "I know you're that, but what am I?"

Douglas Haig: "DO YOU HAVE ANY LAST ORDERS BEFORE I ASSUME COMMAND?"

John French: "No need to raise your voice, old bean. Yes, I would like Winston Churchill to be given command of a Brigade in France?"

Douglas Haig: "I'll do what I can but the best he can expect is his Colonelcy and command of an Infantry Battalion. After that Dardanelle's debacle the War Office is reluctant to put him in charge of the Salvation Army. I won't make the same mistakes as you two - and I'll get this whole thing wrapped up very quickly, no matter what the cost."

John French: "Yes! Well good luck in achieving that, chummy. Oh by the way, someone told me the other day that you and one of your nags tried to finish the King off, any truth in the matter?"

Douglas Haig: "How dare you poke fun at the Kings' injuries! It was purely an accident and I very much regret that I was partially responsible for the pain caused to his spine, but the horse is to blame!"

John French: "Well...we've all been there. Most of us have suffered a back injury because of you, but ours was due to a knifing incident, anyway, unlike you at least the King has a spine."

Douglas Haig: "That's it - I'm telling!"

6. CAPTAIN CHAVASSE AND PRIVATE RATCLIFFE
(THE SOMME – 1916)

Noel Godfrey Chavasse was one of twins born in Oxford on the 9th of November 1884. Maybe Noel and his brother Christopher were pre-destined to follow in the family tradition of becoming either men of medicine, or men of the cloth. Their father, the Reverend Francis James Chavasse, eventually became the Bishop of Liverpool and himself followed a long line of Chavasse family men who became Doctors and Vicars. Noel would turn to medicine whilst his twin, Christopher, went into the Church. In the 1908 Olympic Games they both competed in the 400 meter race, but failed to qualify for the final stages.

When the Chavasse family moved to Liverpool, Noel qualified both as a doctor and surgeon at the Liverpool Royal Southern Hospital. In 1913 he joined the 10th (Scottish) Battalion of The King's Liverpool Regiment, serving as their Regimental Medical Officer. When on the 4th of August 1914 Britain declared war on Germany, the Territorial 'Scousers' were called up with other units to form part of the BEF (British Expeditionary Force). The 10th King's Liverpool Battalion set sail from Southampton on the 3rd of November 1914, heading for France. Noel was now destined to become one of the most famous Officers ever to have served in the British Army, but fate decreed that he would never return to his family in England.

Noel Godfrey was a man ahead of his time as far as Army medicine was concerned. He was different from most of the Army doctors who had been called up into the ranks of the RAMC (Royal Army Medical Corps). He held sick parades every morning whether the Battalion was in the front line trenches, in the support trenches just behind the front line or if they were taking a rest back in the Corps areas. He was constantly proactive in the Battalions soldier's welfare. When they came out of the line he made sure that hot baths and food were made available for them as soon as they reached their rest area. The Chavasse family back at home in Liverpool also helped Noel in all ways answering his never ending appeals for 'soldier comforts.' They once answered his request for a gramophone and records which were then loaned to each Company for a given time. The Bishop and his wife also answered Noel

Godfrey's request for over 1000 woollen socks to help keep the men's feet warm, dry, and healthy. These were gifted to the men when Noel's team of medics went round each Company carrying out foot inspections. Soldiers showing signs of trench foot were treated immediately, in the hope that the damage was limited and their recovery time would be minimalized. Those found with trench foot were not threatened with military discipline, they were treated and given advice.

During his Battalions' time under fire in the trenches, Captain Chavasse could be found treating casualties in his RAP (Regimental Aid Post), or running around no-man's land, picking up the wounded and bringing them back to the safety of the British trenches. He didn't expect his stretcher-bearers to do anything that he wouldn't do himself. Shell Shock was the buzz word of the First World War and any of Noel's soldiers who were suffering from it were employed at his Regimental Aid Post for a short time helping with the wounded. He understood that they weren't cowards and that they'd simply reached the end of their mental tether. They all needed some sort of re-assurance, comfort, and time to recover. If he recognised that in the early stages of the war, then it begs the question - why didn't any of the other Officers have the intelligence to understand the problem and the courage to stand up to the Top Brass?

Compare this to Captain Harry Dearden RAMC who attended a Court Martial to give medical evidence for a deserter captured behind the lines (the soldier was more than likely suffering from Shell Shock). In his book 'Medicine and Duty,' Dearden explained, "I went to the trial determined to give him no help of any sort, for I detest his type; and seeing so many good fellows go out during the night's shelling made me all the more bitter against him for trying to back down. I really hoped he would be shot, as indeed was anticipated by all of us." At the trial, Dearden lost his bottle when he saw the soldier "looking so hopelessly forlorn and lonely," and so he tried to let him down slowly. He told the Court Martial that the soldier was "a man he considered was much below the standard of the ordinary man in every way mentally." The soldier was acquitted of the charge but Dearden thought at the time, "He'll never make anything, and will probably bolt again the first chance he gets. They tell me he'll probably get shot by his own mates the next time we go over the top, so a bright outlook anyway, poor devil."

In a similar case, Captain Noel Godfrey Chavasse was put under pressure to condemn an accused soldier, but he refused to 'gang up' on the sick and frightened man, much to the annoyance of his fellow Officers and Gentlemen. Because he was vocally critical of the Royal Army Medical Corps' attitude and procedures, he wasn't promoted above the rank of Captain. Here was a strong willed and compassionate man who could definitely think 'outside the box.' At

Guillemont on the Somme on the 24th of October 1916, Noel Godfrey won the first of his two Victoria Crosses (VC). By this time he'd already been awarded an MC (Military Cross). His Citation was published on 24th October 1916 and read:

Captain Noel Godfrey Chavasse MC, M.B, Royal Army Medical Corps.
For most conspicuous bravery and devotion to duty.

During an attack he attended to the wounded in the open all day, under heavy fire, frequently in view of the enemy. During the ensuing night he searched for wounded on the ground in front of the enemy's lines for four hours.

Next day he took one stretcher-bearer to the advanced trenches, and under heavy shell fire carried an urgent case for 500 yards into safety, being wounded in the side by a shell splinter during the journey. The same night he took up a party of twenty volunteers, rescued three wounded men from a shell hole twenty five yards from the enemy trench, buried the bodies of two Officers, and collected many identity discs, although fired on by bombs and machine guns.

Although he saved the lives of some twenty badly wounded men, besides the ordinary cases which passed through his hands, were beyond praise.

As if winning an MC (Military Cross) and a VC (Victoria Cross) wasn't enough, Noel Godfrey went on to win a Bar to his Victoria Cross on 2nd August 1917 at Wieltje in Belgium. This citation was published on 14th September 1917 and read:

His Majesty the King has been graciously pleased to approve of the award of a Bar to the Victoria Cross to Captain Noel Godfrey Chavasse VC, MC, late RAMC, attached to 10th (Scottish) Battalion of The King's Liverpool Regiment.

For most conspicuous bravery and devotion to duty when in action.

Though severely wounded early in the action whilst carrying a wounded soldier to the Dressing Station, Captain Chavasse refused to leave his post, and for two days not only continued to perform his duties, but in addition went out repeatedly under heavy fire to search and attend to the wounded who were lying out.

During these searches, although practically without food during this period, worn with fatigue and faint with his wound, he assisted to carry in a number of badly wounded men, over heavy and difficult ground.

By his extraordinary energy and inspiring example, he was instrumental in rescuing many wounded who would otherwise undoubtedly succumbed under the bad weather conditions.

This devoted and gallant Officer subsequently died of his wounds.

Since it came into being on 29th January 1856, only three men have ever won a Victoria Cross and Bar. The other two winners were Lieutenant Arthur Martin-Leake of the Royal Army Medical Corps, who won his first VC during the Second Boer War in 1902 and his second VC at Zonnebeke in 1914. Captain Charles Upham was a New Zealand Infantry Officer who won both of his VC's during the Second World War, his first on the island of Crete in 1941 and the second in Egypt in 1942. Co-incidentally, Lieutenant Martin-Leake was a doctor serving with 46th Field Ambulance, which was the unit that brought Noel Godfrey back to Brandhoek Dressing Station just before he died, and Captain Charles Upham was related to the Chavasse family by marriage.

It seems sacrilegious to try and put words into the mouth of this supreme humanitarian, but we do so in the hope that you the reader will understand that we are simply trying to emulate how Noel Godfrey might have treated the soldiers under his care. Picture the scene in the 10th King's Liverpool Battalions' Regimental Aid Post in the front line during 1916:

Stretcher Bearer 1: "Sir, we've got another one here, he's bleeding quite heavily from his thigh. I think it's a through and through wound sir."

Noel Godfrey: "Ok, put some extra pressure on that shell dressing and I'll see to him in a minute."

Stretcher Bearer 1: "Will do sir."

Noel Godfrey: "Right lad, I've put a firm dressing on your stomach and the morphia will help with the pain. Sergeant! We need to get this chap away to the CCS (Casualty Clearing Station) as soon as possible."

Sergeant: "Leave it to me sir. Right, you two lads get hold of this stretcher and take him back to the CCS. Make sure you come straight back mind, and don't forget to bring a replacement stretcher with you. Be quick about it as well!"

Stretcher Bearer 1: "I've stopped the bleeding sir, but the blood pisses out as soon as I take the pressure off. What do you want me to do?"

Noel Godfrey: "Let's have a look at him. Hmmm...I think you may have a nicked artery there my lad. Nothing to worry about though, the surgeons will repair it and leave you with a nice little scar you can tell your mates about. Pass me a tourniquet and a fresh shell dressing, will you Sergeant? This is going to be a bit painful lad and you must make sure the tourniquet is released about every fifteen minutes, can you remember that?"

Casualty: "Yes sir, every fifteen minutes. Am I going to lose my leg Doctor...I mean sir?"

Noel Godfrey: "Ha Ha, not over a small scratch like that, no need to worry, you'll be fine. Sergeant, let's give him a couple of grains of morphia to slow down his heart rate and reduce the bleeding."

After applying the tourniquet and administering the morphia the last stretcher is removed from the dugout and the stretcher bearers head off to the Casualty Clearing Station (CCS). In the corner of the dugout a soldier is shaking and looks very distressed, he's covered in blood.

Noel Godfrey: "Sergeant, is that young Private Ratcliffe?"

Sergeant: "Yes sir, he just walked in with the other casualties."

Noel Godfrey: "Are you ok young Ratcliffe, are you in pain or bleeding?"

Private Ratcliffe: "No sir."

Noel Godfrey: "Tell me what happened to you?"

Private Ratcliffe: "Me and two of me mates were in a sap trench when a shell landed near us...Stan was killed outright and I got covered in his blood...he never had a chance sir...the shell took half his head off sir."

Noel Godfrey: "What about your other friend, was he killed as well?"

Private Ratcliffe: "No sir, Kenny took some shrapnel in his chest and started coughing up blood...I did what I could for him...put a shell dressing on like you told us to do, I think he's dead sir. I didn't have the strength to carry him back."

Noel Godfrey: "Where is the sap trench located?"

Private Ratcliffe: "About thirty metres into No-man's Land, just in front of where we are now sir."

Noel Godfrey: "Well done lad, you've done everything you possibly could. My Sergeant is going to give you a hot sweet cup of tea now and you need to have a chat with him -, and don't worry we're going to find your friends and bring them both back in."

Private Ratcliffe: "I tried to save Kenny sir, but I think he just died. It wasn't my fault...he always looked out for me did Kenny, but I just couldn't save him...I really did try sir...but I didn't know what else I could do...I think he died sir."

Noel Godfrey: "I'm sure you did all you could young Ratcliffe. I don't think even a Doctor could have saved him. He would have been comforted that you were with him when he died, at least he wasn't alone."

Private Ratcliffe: "I tried to save him sir, I did what you taught us during those lessons but I think he died sir...I didn't know what else to do sir...I think he died sir."

Noel Godfrey: "Ok Private Ratcliffe, I do understand. You stay here and rest a while and I'll go and find your friends."

Private Ratcliffe: "I tried to save him sir...I really did."

Noel Godfrey: "Sergeant! Keep a close eye on Private Ratcliffe while I'm out. You're in charge of the Regimental Aid Post (RAP) until I get back. Corporal! Grab three stretcher bearers and a couple of stretchers, we're going to find Private Ratcliffe's friends."

7. BARON VON RICHTHOFEN
AND
CAPTAIN ARTHUR ROY BROWN
(THE SOMME – 1918)

Manfred Albrecht von Richthofen (born on 2 May 1892 - died on 21 April 1918) is probably best remembered as being 'The Red Baron,' a German fighter pilot with the Imperial German Army Air Service during the First World War. He was officially credited with eighty air combat victories and was bestowed with many German plaudits. In January 1917, after his 16th confirmed kill, Von Richthofen was awarded the Pour le Merit (better known as "The Blue Max").

Originally a cavalryman, Richthofen transferred to the Air Service in 1915, quickly distinguishing himself as an outstanding, and naturally gifted fighter pilot. In 1917 he became leader of what eventually developed into his "Flying Circus." Von Richthofen recruited only the bravest and most skilled pilots into his 'Jastas' (Fighter Squadrons) and they copied his idea of painting their aircraft in the gaudiest of colours (Von Richthofen's Fokker Dr.1 Triplane being red) so that they were easily identifiable whilst flying. By 1918 Manfred Von Richthofen had achieved an almost God-like reputation, both at home and abroad.

Richthofen was eventually shot down and killed near Amiens on the 21st of April 1918. There has been considerable debate over the circumstances of his death. It was initially believed he had been shot down by Captain Arthur Roy Brown RNAS (Royal Naval Air Service) but there is now a school of thought that believes he may have been brought down by an Australian Army Machine-Gunner. When fatally wounded and in the last few minutes of his life, he managed to make a hasty but controlled landing on a hill near the Bray-Corbie road, just north of the village of Vaux-sur-Somme, a sector that was under the control of the Australian Imperial Force (AIF). Gunner George Ridgway, stated that when he and other Australian soldiers reached the red aircraft, the pilot was still alive but died a few moments later. Von Richthofen is still regarded by any as being one of the finest and bravest fighter pilots of all time.

Captain Arthur Roy Brown was a pilot serving in the Royal Naval Air Service (RNAS) during World War One and was credited with shooting down the 'Red Baron,' although this victory is still strongly debated. On the day Von Richthofen was shot down, Captain Brown dived toward the ground to help a comrade who was being chased by the 'Red Baron.' The confrontation was only brief because after firing a short burst from his machine guns, Brown had to pull up to avoid crashing into the ground. He then lost contact with the other two aircraft and headed back to his own airfield. On hearing of the death of Baron Von Richthofen, Captain Brown went to pay his respects to the body of the greatest pilot the world had ever known, "There was a lump in my throat as if he had been my dearest friend. I could not have felt any greater sorrow." Such was his respect for this warrior pilot. Captain Brown was awarded a Bar to his DSC (Distinguished Service Cross) in recognition of his part in this action.

The following conversations could well have taken place both before and after the death of 'The Red Baron':

Brown: "Right chaps, I'm going to sort this bugger 'The Red Baron' and his colleagues out once and for all. They're a damned nuisance. I've got a jolly good idea where he's lurking."

Sergeant: "Well your aircraft is good to go, sir."

Brown: "Excellent, I'll get cracking straight away and be back in no time at all. Get the chaps to swing the old girl's tail around into the wind, will you."

Sergeant: "Certainly sir. How long are you likely to be up for, sir?"

Brown: "Oh, not too long. I'll try and bag a couple of the buggers though before breakfast!"

Sergeant: "I'll warn cook off. He's had a delivery of fresh eggs this morning."

Brown: "That's champion! Tally Ho!"

Sergeant: "Go get the German bastard, sir!"

Brown: "Steady on Sergeant, remember that you're talking about an Officer and a Gentleman!"

Sergeant: "Sorry sir, it won't happen again."

Brown: "Not if I catch the German bastard it won't! Chocks away!"

Captain Brown laughed and took off. Meanwhile back at Von Richthofen's 'Flying Circus.'

Von Richthofen: "I think that it is high time the English 'Ace' Captain Brown was brought down to earth with a bang! I know he's in the area somewhere, he has been spotted. I am going to seek him out. Is my aircraft ready, Feldwebel?"

Feldwebel: "Jawhoul, Herr Hauptmann, she is fully armed and fuelled."

Von Richthofen: "Excellent. Let's see if I can increase my score then. Hah – you'd better watch your tail – Captain Brown! What a lovely day this is. "

Later on, the Red Baron's Aircraft lands in a field, rolling to a stop in one corner, its engine still running. Slumped in the cockpit is a fatally wounded Von Richthofen. Australian Gunner, Gunner Ridgway sees the halted aircraft, realises that something is amiss and decides to capture the pilot.

Gunner Ridgway: "Here, I recognise that aircraft – it's the bloody Red Baron. Bugger me, cheeky sod's landed right over there, come on, let's go and nab him before he gets a chance to take off again!"

Ridgway ran across to the aircraft, the propeller is still turning, the pilot slumped in his seat. Ridgway pointed his rifle at the Pilot.

Gunner Ridgway: "Oy! You'd better switch that engine off, then get your hands up, you krout bastard! You're not going anywhere else today! "

The pilot smiled at Ridgway and spoke just one word.

Von Richthofen: "Kaput!"

He then slumped forward.

Gunner Ridgway: "That's torn it. I think he's been shot!"

Standing behind Gunner Ridgway is Medical Sergeant Ted Smout.

Gunner Ridgway: "Sarn't Smout, you'd better come and take a look at him. He's bleeding like a stuck pig!"

Sergeant Smout: "Out of the way Gunner, let the dog see the bone!"

The Medical Sergeant examines Von Richthofen.

Sergeant Smout: "It's no good mate, I'm afraid he's had it. Bullet through the chest. Can't do anything for him now, he's dead! Let's lift him out of the aircraft."

Gunner Ridgway: "Is he the Red Baron, Sarge? Let's take his flying helmet off and have a look."

They gently removed Von Richthofen's flying helmet.

Sergeant Smout: "Yes, It's 'The Red Baron' all right. I've seen photos of him. Cor, look at his bloody gongs! That one's the 'Blue Max!' Hell fire cobber, we've snagged the Red Baron!"

Gunner Ridgway: "Not much cop if he's docked his clogs, is it, Sarge!"

Sergeant Smout: "Suppose not. One thing's for sure though, he won't be shooting any more of our chaps down."

Gunner Ridgway: "Here Sarge, he said something to me just before he died."

Sergeant Smout: "Oh yeah, what was that?"

Gunner Ridgway: "Just one word, he said, 'Kaput.' What does Kaput mean, Sarge?"

Sergeant Smout: "I don't know the precise meaning mate, but I think it means he's well and truly buggered. Let's see if we can switch the aircraft engine off. It's giving me a bloody headache."

8. QUEEN ELIZABETH AND BENITO MUSSOLINI
(ROME - 1938)

We don't suppose there is much we can tell you about the Queen Mum. Let's face it, she has been filmed, photographed and written about since the day she was born into the British Nobility. But here we go with a few facts and figures.

Elizabeth Angela Marguerite Bowes-Lyon (born on the 4th of August 1900 and died on the 30th of March 2002). This feisty woman married Prince Albert, the Duke of York, who happened to be the second son of King George V. Edward VIII was Crowned King on the death of his father King George V, but abdicated from the throne in 1936 to marry Wallace Simpson, a divorced American woman, (boo, hiss, she's behind you)! This was deemed completely unacceptable (quite right too) to everyone in the Royal Household and the Government of the day. Consequently Prince Albert stepped up to the plate. He assumed the mantle and became King George VI, subsequently, his wife Elizabeth became Queen of Great Britain, Ireland and the British Dominions, and Empress of India, on the 12th May 1937. Elizabeth accompanied her husband on diplomatic tours before the start of the Second World War. Adolf Hitler described her as being "the most dangerous woman in Europe." The Queen Mother was, sadly, widowed at the age of 51 when King George VI died in 1952; it was in the same year that her first born, Princess Elizabeth, was crowned Queen Elizabeth II. The Queen Mum became known as Queen Elizabeth the Queen Mother in order to avoid any misdirection of the mail sent to her daughter.

Footnote: When Brian (Harry) Clacy was working as a Civil Servant in York he became good friends with an ex-Regimental Sergeant Major (RSM) of the Irish Guards called Sammy Connors. This wonderful man worked for the Defence Housing Establishment and was of the 'old school,' which meant that he always swore like a Guardsman with his trousers on fire. No offence was ever meant by Sammy because when he effed and blinded, he was merely using the words as adjectives.

Sammy once told Harry that when he was the RSM of his Battalion he was organising the annual Warrant Officers' and Sergeant's Mess photograph on St

Patrick's Day. The Queen Mum was presenting all Mess Members with a traditional piece of fresh shamrock before joining in with them for the Mess photograph. Whilst organising the seating positions of his Mess Members, WO 1 (RSM) Sammy Connors shouted across the Mess to a Guardsman he had posted on the main entrance door, "Keep your fucking eyes peeled young man! I want you to let me know when the fucking Queen Mother arrives!" From the door behind him the Queen mum suddenly and unexpectedly entered the Mess and announced in a posh voice, "Mr Connors, the fucking Queen Mother has arrived!"

Benito Mussolini

(With his mate Adolf)

Benito Mussolini (born 29th July 1883 and died on the 28th of April 1945). He was the Prime Minister of Italy and leader of the National Fascist Party there from 1922 until 1943, when the Grand Council of Fascism voted against him and he was ousted from power. 'Il Duce' (The Leader), as he liked to be called, was imprisoned by the Italian Fascist Government but his prison location was kept secret from the occupying German Army. The Italian Government thought that Adolf Hitler might attempt to free him because Mussolini was allied to the Third Reich before and during World War Two. The Fascist Party were right to be worried because that is exactly what happened. After being held in captivity for two months, an elite German Fallschirmjager (Paratrooper) unit planned and executed a dramatic mountain top rescue of Il Duce. After releasing the Italian dictator from his prison cell they then flew him off the mountain in a glider and he was restored to some sort of power in Northern Italy by Adolf Hitler. In April 1945 the war in Europe was virtually over, all bar the shouting, and the majority of the Italian Forces had swopped sides and were assisting the Allies. Benito Mussolini realised the game was up and tried to make his escape to Spain via Switzerland. Italian partisans captured Mussolini and his mistress, Clara Petacci, along with some of his cronies and they were all swiftly tried and executed. Their bodies were hung upside down at an Esso garage where all and sundry viewed and abused the corpses, something of an unseemly end.

48

Before the start of the Second World War, the Duke of York and Elizabeth were due to attend an Italian Royal wedding in Rome. Elizabeth couldn't attend because she was feeling unwell at the time (she was in fact newly pregnant with Princess Margaret) and so her husband had to unhappily travel and be present on his own. Because of this Elizabeth never actually had the 'pleasure' of meeting Il Duce, but if they had then our wonderful Queen Mother to be, with her love of the Scottish people and their language, may have had a chat similar something along these lines:

Elizabeth: "Keep the heid and gizza minute to neck this G & T then send him in. Oh and shut that window on your way out will ye, it's as cold as a witches tit in here! Why they call it them French windows when we're in Italy I'll never ken."

"**Ambassador:** "As you wish Ma'am."

The Ambassador closes the French window and exits walking backwards. He backs into the doorframe with a resultant loud crash.

Elizabeth: "Easy tiger, ye startled me…nearly spilt ma shwally!"

Ambassador: "Forgive me Ma'am, I didn't mean to startle you."

Elizabeth: "You're going to have to get a hang o' the walking backwards bit ye ken, on yer way noo, there's a good wee chappie."

Ambassador: "Certainly Ma'am. Should I send Mr Mussolini in?"

Elizabeth: "Aye yer may as well. Bugger it, I've spilt most o' ma shwally. I'll get another wee dram when he comes in, it'll help tae break the ice n'that, eh!"

The Ambassador exits to summon Benito Mussolini.

Elizabeth: "He's a strange wee laddie that Ambassador. Told me he was brought up at Eton! Looks as if he was Eton and brought up more like! Where's ma bleedin' sporran."

Elizabeth opens her sporran and takes out a packet of cigarettes. There's a knock on the door and the Ambassador announces the arrival of Benito Mussolini.

Ambassador: "Ma'am, may I present Mr Benito Mussolini."

Mussolini enters the room and bows.

Mussolini: "Ah, Ma'am, it is such a pleasure to meet you."

Elizabeth: "Aye I ken. Come on in and set yersel doon on the chaise longue aside me, pal."

Elizabeth patted the silk cushions that surrounded her. Mussolini joins her on the chaise longue. Because he is rather small, his legs dangle and don't quite reach the floor. He sits there swinging them like a little schoolboy. Elizabeth offers him a cigarette from her packet of Woodbines.

Elizabeth: "Yon's cracking pair o' boots hen! Mind the couch with those spurs will yer, wee mawn!"

Mussolini: "Ma'am."

Elizabeth: "A wee fag?"

Mussolini is outraged.

Mussolini: "I beg your pardon Madam! I am as straight as a die!"

Elizabeth: "No, no, och ma head's mince, I mean would you like a smoke, mayhap a Woodbine!"

Mussolini: "No thank you, Ma'am, I only smoke cheroots."

Elizabeth: "Well, I'm going tae have a gasper if ye dinna mind."

She lights a cigarette and has a hearty cough.

Elizabeth: "Whisht, these coffin nails will be the death o' me!"

Mussolini: "Forgive me Ma'am, but you are more beautiful than I could ever have imagined. Your skin is flawless, your eyes are like pools and your teeth are like stars. Your husband, the Duke, is indeed a most fortunate man to have you at his side. Would that I were so fortunate."

Elizabeth laughs and slaps her thigh.

Elizabeth: "My eyes are like pools – aye futtba pools! Ma teeth are like stars – aye, they come oot at night! Haud yer shite wee fellow! Och, you Eyetalians, such charmers. Here, fancy a wee splash, Benito?"

Mussolini: "No, I went before I came in."

Elizabeth: "No, no – a splash – a drink – a bevvy!"

Mussolini: "Oh, forgive me Ma'am. My command of English leaves a little to be desired."

Elizabeth: "Och aye, well so does my Italian, dear. A Gin and Tonic do you?"

Mussolini: "That would be 'spiffing' - as you English say."

Elizabeth: "Cheeky! Less o' the English or I'll gie ye a skelpit lug! One is a Jock through an' through! Come on, let's get this booze sorted."

She rings a hand bell and a Manservant enters.

Elizabeth: "Ah, Steven, pour me and Mr Mussolini a G & T each will yer, there's a good wee laddie. By the way, Steven, love the Simmet!"

Servant: "Why, thank you Ma'am."

The Manservant poured two Gin and Tonics and served them from a silver salver to Elizabeth and Mussolini.

Elizabeth: "Cheers pal. On yer way now – oh, and Steven..."

Servant: "Ma'am."

Elizabeth: "Ease back on the lipstick and eye-shadow, eh, there's a good wee lad. Yer eyelids are as black as the Earl of Hell's waistcoat! Bit over the top, if ye get ma drift. You'll never pull looking like that!"

Servant: "Ma'am."

The servant exits.

Elizabeth: "Noo then Mr Mussolini. Our meeting, you asked to see me, so what's it all aboot n'that?"

Mussolini: "Ma'am, I thought that it would be an ideal opportunity, whilst you are visiting here, to discuss the friendship between our two Nations at the highest of levels and with a degree of privacy."

Elizabeth: "Och, did they not tell you? I cannae get involved in that sort o' shite. I'm apolitical. I just open things, cut ribbons, n'stuff like that. Anything else and I'd get a good skelpin.' Ma old man does all o' that wheelin' an' dealin' crap. He's oot doing a bit of skiing at the mo'. Have you been oot on the piste?"

Mussolini: "No Ma'am, not a drop has passed my lips. This is my first today!"

Elizabeth laughs and slaps Mussolini's thigh.

Elizabeth: "Och you are such a wag, Benito. You dinna mind me calling you Benito, do you hen?"

Mussolini: "Please do, Ma'am. It's an honour."

Elizabeth: "Aye, well it's the only honour you'll be getting frae us, eh!

Mussolini grasps Elizabeth's hand.

Mussolini: "May I, er, call you Elizabeth?"

She pulls her hand free and gives Mussolini a stinging blow on his head.

Elizabeth: "You'd better nae de that again, Benny boy! Why, we've only just met. Just remember your position in the scheme of things, eh pal! Me Royal, you commoner! Only my old man gets to use ma first name, geddit ye big bawface?"

Mussolini: "Forgive me, Ma'am."

Elizabeth: "That's more like it. A wee tad of subservience goes a long way. Another dram?"

Mussolini: "But I haven't finished this one yet, Ma'am."

Elizabeth: "Well knock it back then, hen. The sun's over the yard arm! We can sink a couple more whilst we're sat here blethering. You're stopping on for a wee while longer aren't ye?"

Mussolini: "Alas, no Ma'am, I have to fly to Berlin to meet the Fuhrer, Herr Hitler this evening."

Elizabeth: "Oh him, rayght. Drap of business goin' doon is it?"

Elizabeth rings a hand bell. The Manservant enters. She nods sagely at the drinks cabinet. He pours two more drinks, serves them and then exits.
Elizabeth: "So, you're away to see that balmpot Herr Hitler are ye?"

Mussolini: "Yes Ma'am."

Elizabeth: "Aye, well do give the wee scunner my regards will you – and tell him that his moustache makes him look like Charlie Chaplin! Bloody ridiculous, he should let it grow or shave it off. And that wee fringe of his needs trimming! It's like a curtain! What a man! He'd benefit from a wee boot up the Bahooky."

Benito is by this time getting a little pissed, particularly as he'd had a large glass of brandy before meeting Elizabeth. He laughs out loud at Elizabeth's moustache comment.

Mussolini: "Ha Ha – I shall certainly broach the subject with the Fuhrer, if that is your wish."

Elizabeth: "Aye, go on, and tell him that if he doesnae shut his geggie, he's going to get a swift kick in the Wallies frae the Brits!"

Mussolini: "Ma'am?"

Elizabeth: "I'm nae much cop at this diplomatic lingo but I'm sure he'll get ma drift, ken. Tell him to be a good boy, stop within his own borders and stay at hame n' everything will be just tickety boo. No more 'Lebensraum!' Simple as that."

Mussolini: "Your wish is my desire, Ma'am."

Benito belches ferociously. There's a distinct whiff of garlic.

Elizabeth: "Och, Christ, has the cat deid! What the hell hay yew bin aytin, ma man?"

Mussolini: "Is Garlic. Forgive me, Ma'am."

Elizabeth: "Christ, I'd give the old garlic a wee body swerve if I were you Benny boy! Ye ken, we've all got to make a bleedin living but that Adolf's just taking the pish! I've seen the newsreels and how he's building his Navy and

Luftwaffe up! We've hoisted in what's going on! It's high time he shut his geggie."

Mussolini: "I thought that you would have been pleased to see a stronger Germany, Ma'am. Are you not of German descent yourself?"

Elizabeth grabs Mussolini by his lapels and clouts him.

Elizabeth: "Noo jist hod on a wee moment, pal! I told ye that I'm a Jock! Less o' the Krout crap, eh or you'll be getting a taste o' the heed! Now, ease back and have a nippie sweetie!"

Mussolini: "Well Ma'am, just one more drink then I must, as they say, hit the road."

Elizabeth: "Jeez Bennie, I hope you're nae behint the wheel! Ye shouldnae be driving when you're pished!"

Mussolini: "Ah no Ma'am, I have a car and driver. It is a beautiful Mercedes Benz, presented to me personally by Herr Hitler actually."

Elizabeth: "A wee word o' warnin' Ben. You start taking backhanders frae that wee shite bag an' yew'll be headin' for a wee spot o' grief. There's nae such thing as a free lunch you know. Wee Adolf is a sleekit bastard. It'll only end in tears, ma wee fellow."

Mussolini: "I will keep a watchful eye out for that, Ma'am."

He discreetly examines his watch.

Mussolini: "Forgive me Ma'am but regrettably I must take my leave of you."

Elizabeth: "Och, gizza break n'that! We're just getting to know one n'other. Tell ye what, ye must come ower tae London and pay us a visit. Bring wee Adolf n'all if yer like, ye ken. I mean just tae visit, not to invade!"

Elizabeth laughs loudly. Benito flinched, expecting another blow to the head. She rings her bell. The Ambassador returns.

Elizabeth: "Ah Ambassador, Mr Mussolini is on his way oot. Gie him a hond will ye. He's a wee bit pished."
Mussolini: "Hey Ambassador, I'm a bit, how you say, pished as three sheets."

Elizabeth: "Nae problem pal, The Ambassador will see you to your Merc. Nice meeting ye, Bennie and dinnae forget, try and come ower to oor spot and we can have another wee sesh. I'll get ma Chef to knock up a nice Spag Bol, make you feel right at home, you ken!"

Mussolini: "You are most considerate, Ma'am. I bid you a fond farewell."
He moves forward and attempts to his Elizabeth's hand. She slaps him on the head.

Elizabeth: "Er, well have none of that, ye ken!"

The Ambassador and Mussolini both exit, walking backwards, the Ambassador sniggering and Mussolini rubbing his head.

Mussolini: "Mr Ambassador, why do we have to exit backwards?"

Ambassador: "Haven't got a bloody clue old bean, other than that you must never turn your back on Royalty."

Mussolini laughs.

Mussolini: "Having seen her manservant I know just what you mean!"

The Queen calls out to Mussolini.

Elizabeth: "I enjoyed our wee blether, Ben. Haste ye back! Oh and lang may yer lum reek!"

Mussolini: "You know, Ambassador, she kept calling me Ben and then Ken. I don't understand?"

They both exit.

Elizabeth: "Jeez, what a scunner! Och, it's the worst part o' the job meeting these bloody foreigners. Better get changed into me evening frock before ma wee Georgie gets back, he's bound to be a bit crabbit. I might put a bit more slap on. Another little splash of G & T afore I make tracks - madness not to."

9. WINSTON CHURCHILL AND CHARLES DE GAULLE
(LONDON - 1940)

General Charles André Joseph Marie de Gaulle was the dominant military and political leader of France for much of the period from 1940 to 1969. He refused to accept his government's truce/surrender with/to the invading German Army in 1940. After setting up a temporary French capital in London he declared himself the incarnation of France and created the Free French movement. In 1944 he became the leader of the French Provisional Government after its liberation from the Third Reich.

He also became the leader of the Provisional Government of France following its liberation in 1944 and is believed to have been the strongest and greatest of French leaders since Napoleon Bonaparte. De Gaulle led a Government in exile and the Free French Forces (composed of French soldiers in Britain) against France's pro-German Vichy government. His promotion of French national interests eventually led to confrontations with the 'Big Three' Allied leaders, Churchill, Stalin and Roosevelt, especially Franklin D Roosevelt and the U.S., due to the uncertain status of France before the Liberation.

Sir Winston Leonard Spencer Churchill is widely regarded as having been one of the greatest wartime leaders of the 20th century. Churchill was born into the aristocratic family of the Duke of Marlborough. As a young army officer, he saw action in British India, the Sudan, and the Second Boer War. He took the lead in warning about Nazi Germany and in campaigning for rearmament. At the outbreak of the Second World War, he was appointed First Lord of the Admiralty, a signal being issued from the Admiralty which read "Winston is back."

Following the resignation of Neville Chamberlain on 10 May 1940, Churchill became Prime Minister. His steadfast refusal to consider defeat, surrender, or a compromise peace helped inspire British resistance, especially during the difficult early days of the war when the British Commonwealth and Empire stood alone in its active opposition to Adolf Hitler. Churchill led Britain as Prime Minister until victory over Nazi Germany and Japan had been secured.

In the summer of 1943, de Gaulle, who had escaped to London in 1940 after the fall of France, became undisputed leader of the Free French, ending Churchill's attempts to have him removed. Thoughts of abandoning de Gaulle were made difficult because of the agreement Churchill had signed with him in 1940. At that time Britain faced invasion by the Germans and Churchill desperately needed the help of the incredibly brave French Resistance. De Gaulle continued to lead the French Resistance movement from his base in London until France was liberated in 1944.

This conversation may have taken place at Number 10 Downing Street, London. Wartime Leader, Winston Churchill had sent for General de Gaulle to discuss events leading up to 'D Day.' They didn't like or trust each other. Winston was full of false bonhomie.

Winston: "Ah, Chas, come on in my old son. Grab le pew."

Charles: "Le pew?"

Winston: "Yes, I mean Oui. Pull up a chaise longue and park yer carcase."

Charles: "Merci, Monsieur Churchill."

Winston: "Fancy a wet?"

Charles: "Pardon?"

Winston: "A wet, a gargle…you know…a drink?"

Charles: "That would be most civilised. A glass of chilled Chardonnay, perhaps?"

Winston: "You're taking the piss int yer? There's a bleedin war on in case you'd forgotten. I've got a nice crate of London Pride brahn ale in for us. That'll have to do."

Charles: "Bon, needs must when le devil drives."

Winston opens a couple of bottles of beer and pours them.

Winston: "Sorry abaht the tin mugs, Chas. As I said, there's a war on! Cheers!"

They drink the brown ale, De Gaulle gags.

Charles: "Merde, but that is how would you say – different!   But oui, I know, there is a war on, n'est pas!"

There's a sound of rustling paper. Winston hands de Gaulle a small, greasy brown paper bag.

Winston: "Pork scratching, my dear?"

Charles: "Non! Not for me, Prime Minister. Pork scratching's are a strangely English tradition."

Winston: "Bugger all strange abaht the old pork scratchings Chas. Go dahn well with a drop of the old brown ale they do. My driver gets 'em from the NAAFI for me. It's things like pork scratching's that this war is all abaht! Freedom of choice, innit!"

Charles: "Prime Minister, one hates to be boorish, but may I enquire why I have been 'summoned' to your presence?"

Winston: "Easy Chas, you 'ain't been summoned, more like invited. You are, when all's said and done, France's true leader! Not like that shit-house Petain, eh! He'll get his, the two faced toe-rag!"

Charles: "Indeed, Petain will, as you say, get his just desserts. So, why am I here?"

Winston: "I thought that you might like to know that 'D' Day has been brought forward and I wanted to sort out the 'Order of March' in plenty of time for when we eventually reach Paris, which we will!"

Charles: "Le Order de Marche?"

Winston: "Yerst, the Victory Parade dahn the Champs de le Elysee. There's going to be a lot of the world's press there and I don't want you hogging everything? I mean fair's fair, innit! We all deserve dibs."

Charles: "Let me make something perfectly clear Monsieur Churchill, it will be me and my staff who will lead the victory parade when we enter my beloved Paris and march triumphantly along the Champs Elysees. I am the legitimate leader of my beloved France, no-one else. It is only right and proper that I should lead the Victory Parade."

Winston: "Hang on Chas, don't go off on one! What about all we've done for you lot eh? I think that we deserve a place in the front rank. Only fair, innit! We should all get a share of the glory! Let's face it, you'd be speaking kraut if it wasn't for us and the Yanks!"

Charles: "I hear rumours that the American General, Patton, will be leading the advance to Paris! That cannot be allowed. He is an attention seeking cowboy! It would be a circus! No doubt he would like to ride his white stallion whilst twirling his pearl handled pistols! Non Monsieur Churchill, we French must be the first into our beloved Paris, not some gun slinging nincompoop! The honour of La Belle France is at stake!"

Winston: "Don't be so harsh on old George Patton, Chas. Yerst he's a bit of a cowboy but he just likes to, you know, mix it a bit. Here, have another bottle of brahn!"

Charles: "Merci, but non! I must return to my Headquarters and make the necessary plans for my, er, our victorious return to La Belle France!"

Winston: "Not a bad drop of stuff this ale, is it! *(Winston Belches)."*

Charles: "I would have preferred a drop of fine French wine, but as you say, there's a war on."

Winston: "Fair do's. Tell you what, let me have a have a quick chin-wag with Ike abaht all this and I'll give you a bell to confirm. We're all on the same side Chas. Just let yourself out whilst I'll finish this beer old son. Here, I'm expecting a 'phone call from the American President to update me on what's going on across the pond. Better get me head in gear."

Charles: "Very well, Mr Churchill. The fate of my country is in your hands, for the moment."

Winston: "Chas, you've gotta learn to trust me. When all this is over we can get our heads together and sort out Europe once and for all, and don't forget, the bloody Nips have still got to be sorted, mean little bastards they are. I think that the President getting a little something special lined up for them, but I can't talk abaht that just now."

Charles: "I look forward to receiving your telephone call in due course, Prime Minister. Au revoir."

Winston: "TTFN Chas old son!"

General de Gaulle leaves the Prime Minister's office. Churchill picks up the 'phone and reverts to the Queen's English.

Winston: "Eden, pop in here and get rid of this brown ale shite will you, old chap. I'd like a nice Magnum of champagne, a 1930 Delamain Vintage Grand would go down well and two crystal champagne flutes, plenty of ice. Send General Patton in will you, there's something I want to have a chat with him about."

General De Gaulle continued to lead the French resistance movement from Britain until France was liberated in 1944. He led the Victory parade into Paris. Despite his ill-feelings about what he considered to be his derogatory treatment during the war, he was present to pay his respects at Winston Churchill's State funeral on 30th January 1965, after becoming a grudging admirer.

10. ADOLF HITLER
AND
GENERALFELDMARSCHALL PAULUS
(BERLIN/STALINGRAD 1943)

(Both photo's courtesy of the Bundes Archiv)

On the 8th January 1943 the German Sixth Army was virtually surrounded as its soldiers tried, in vain, to capture Stalingrad from the Russian 62nd Army. Adolf Hitler had refused permission for his German soldiers to retreat, even though General Paulus, the Commander of the Sixth Army, had informed him of their desperate situation and his assessment of the inevitable setbacks and rout. The battle had raged on for five of the bloodiest months in the history of warfare, the German soldiers having had to deal with a Russian winter of minus 25 degrees. Because of logistical problems, the Sixth Army was also slowly starving to death. The following telephone conversation between Adolf Hitler (in his nice warm bunker in Berlin) and General Paulus (freezing his nuts off just outside Stalingrad) never took place:

Adolf Hitler: "Hiya Fred, how are things up at the sharp end mate?"

General Paulus: "Mein Fuhrer! I have to report that we are totally surrounded and have lost thousands of men. Those that remain alive are slowly dying from malnutrition and all are suffering from severe frostbite. We cannot continue the fight for much longer!"

Adolf Hitler: "Oh come on Fred, stop being such a drama queen, we'll never win this war with an attitude like that!"

General Paulus: "Mein Fuhrer you must listen to me! We are constantly being bombarded by the Soviet Air Force and artillery, we have very little food left and our stockpiles of ammunition are at a pitiful level. If we don't retreat very soon then I think the Russians will defeat and destroy your magnificent Sixth Army!"

Adolf Hitler: "So you're getting bombarded a couple of times a day, it's not exactly a bleedin' holiday here in Berlin you know. The RAF aren't showering us with love and kisses for Christ's sake! You should see what they've done to my beautiful Berlin, the Bolshevik bastards!!"

General Paulus: "I don't wish to sound like a defeatist, mein Fuhrer but we have very few options left open to us. If only you hadn't assigned our Romanian and Hungarian allies to guard my Northern flank, then things would be very different!"

Adolf Hitler: "Now hold on a second Fred, you're not hanging that shit on me. It's your job to put the troops where you need them, I can't be expected to do everything for you lazy bastards out there! It was only last year that Rommel started bleating about his bloody precious Afrika Korps, "Oh mein Fuhrer, just give me one more Division mein Fuhrer, and I will drive Montgomery out of Egypt, mein Fuhrer." Look what happened then, 'mein bleedin' Fuhrer!' Listen Freddy old son, you'll just have to do the best you can with what you've got and don't let a few Russians grind you down! Just be warned my old son, **no surrender!**"

General Paulus: "But mein Fuhrer…"

Adolf Hitler: "Sorry Freddy I'm going to have to put you on hold for a minute, Martin Bormann, wants to bend my ear about something or other, back in a minute."

Enter a grovelling Martin Bormann, the Nazi Party Secretary.

Martin Bormann: "Guten tag, Boss. I've got a couple of letters that need your flick and I believe you want me to take down some dictation. Do you want me to sit on your knee again?"

Adolf Hitler: "Marty stop taking the piss, I know we have a bit of a laugh now and again but try to remember that I am your Fuhrer."

Martin Bormann: "Forgive me mein Fuhrer. Who's that on the dog and bone?"

Adolf Hitler: "Stalingrad Fred."

Martin Bormann: "Oh Lord, now what's he whinging about?"

Adolf Hitler: "He wants to wave the Italian national flag at the Russians, but I've told him to man up."

Martin Bormann: "You are such an inspirational leader mein Fuhrer. It's a shame that your Generals cannot raise themselves up to match your courage and dedication to the Nationalist cause."

Adolf Hitler: "Get your tongue out of my rear end and back off, Marty. Now, what letters do you want me to sign?"

Martin Bormann: "Rommel has been asking for more concrete so that he can finish building his Atlantic Wall. I believe you have denied his requisition?"

Adolf Hitler: "Too bloody right I have! No-one gets any more concrete until my bunker and that patio out the back are finished."

Martin Bormann: "Jawhoul mein Fuhrer! If you could just sign here…and here… and then put your initials in this space here…and here. Danke schoen mein Fuhrer!"

Adolf Hitler: "What's that other letter for?"

Martin Bormann: "You mentioned last week that General Paulus was whinging about the Stalingrad gig, and that you thought he might be thinking of jacking it in and surrendering to the Russians. Well, the planning committee and I have come up with an idea. Now, in Teutonic history, as you know, no German Generalfeldmarschall has ever surrendered to the enemy, so we thought that if you kicked Paulus upstairs to the top rung he would either have to fight on until he wins the battle or…..well….you know."

Adolf Hitler: "You mean he'd have to top himself. I bloody love it Marty! I could kiss you!"

Martin Bormann: "Oh mein Fuhrer! Well…yeah…that's what the committee thought anyway. Pardon the pun but it kills two birds with one stone. The Reich won't be embarrassed by having one of its Army Commander's surrender and we can publish a story that the Sixth Army continued fighting to the death. Win win as far as we can see."

Adolf Hitler: "That's a work of genius Marty. Do you think he'll fall for it?"

Martin Bormann: "Can't see why not mein Fuhrer, he's old school and will follow any Reich protocol that is put in front of him."

Adolf Hitler: "Living the dream Marty, where do I sign?"

Martin Bormann: "If you could just sign here…here…here and here. That's lovely mein Fuhrer. Do you want to relate the good news to Herr 'General Feldmarshall' Paulus yourself mein Fuhrer?"

Adolf Hitler: "Yep! Leave it to me Mart. Here, tell our Eva to stick the kettle on will you."

Hitler waves Bormann away and continues with the telephone call.

Hitler: "Hello Fred! Are you still on the line mate?"

General Paulus: "Jawhoul mein Fuhrer, I am still here, hanging on by the skin of mein teeth!"

Adolf Hitler: "Nice one Fred, now listen old son, I've got a bit of good news for you. Actually, me, Goering, Himmler and some of the other chaps are really impressed with what you're doing over there in Russia and as a result I've decided to promote you to Generalfeldmarschall with immediate effect. What about that then?"

General Paulus: *(Stunned silence)*

Adolf Hitler: "Hello… you still there Freddie? …I think the line's gone dead. Bloody Bundespost!"

General Paulus: "I'm still here mein Fuhrer. I'm just somewhat surprised at this sudden promotion and, frankly, I'm at a loss as to why you think I'm worthy of it."

Adolf Hitler: "Of course you're worthy of promotion Fred, it's been long overdue, old son."

General Paulus: "Forgive me, but is there some ulterior motive for the rapidity of this promotion, mein Fuhrer?"

Adolf Hitler: "Nah! Leave it out, Have you ever known me try to con anyone?"

General Paulus: "Well yes actually, Neville Chamberlain in 1938 and Marshal Stalin in 1939 are two that spring to mind. You misled the pair of them, and after signing non-aggression pacts you proceeded to send in the Panzers."

Adolf Hitler: "Nobody's perfect Fred. Needs must when the devil drives!"

General Paulus: "I worry that you might be expecting me to…you know…do the honourable thing rather than surrender."

Adolf Hitler: "The honourable thing, Freddie?"

General Paulus: "Commit suicide."

Adolf Hitler: "Freddie, Freddie, as if!"

General Paulus: You are aware that I'm of the Catholic persuasion, mein Fuhrer?"

Adolf Hitler: "What's that got to do with the price of schnitzels?"

General Paulus: "My religious beliefs decree that suicide is a holy sin."

Adolf places his hand over the mouthpiece of the telephone.

Adolf Hitler: "Oh bollocks that's torn it! Hold on a minute Fred. Bormann - get your slack arse back in here!"

Bormann returns, rubbing his hands gratuitously and wearing an ingratiating smile.

Bormann: "Mein Fuhrer?"

Adolf Hitler: "Have we got a 'Plan B' for Stalingrad Fred? He's a bleedin' Catholic, he won't do the suicide thing."

Bormann: "Bloody hell, that buggers things up a bit.   There must be something we can do!"

Adolf Hitler: "I know, give the Vatican a bell!"

Martin Bormann: "Oh that's very witty, mein Fuhrer. Give the Vatican a bell! As if they haven't got enough bells already, neh!"

Adolf Hitler: "See if we can get Freddie some sort of dispensation from Pope Whathisname. Go on then!"

Bormann: "Jawhoul mein Fuhrer. Sieg Heil!"

Bormann exits.
Adolf Hitler: "Cor, have I got to do everything my bleeedin' self around here. Hello Fred, you still there?..... Fred? What's all that noise?"

11. GROUP CAPTAIN DOUGLS BADER
AND
GENERAL ADOLF GALLAND
(COLDITZ CASTLE - 1944)

(Bader photo – Mr S A Devon, RAF Official Photographer)
(Galland photo – Heinrich Hoffmann – Bundes Arciv)

Douglas Bader

Douglas Bader is one of the most famous fighter pilots ever to have climbed into the cockpit of a Spitfire, in fact, he's probably the most celebrated pilot of World War Two, mainly because he didn't have any legs. Bader joined the RAF in 1928 and lost his legs after crashing his aircraft whilst attempting some fancy aerobatics. He was solely responsible for the accident which happened as he was showing off in front of some other RAF pilots. After he'd fully recovered from his double amputations, Douglas went through flight training again, this time wearing his 'Tin Legs.' He passed every flying test and then requested reactivation as an RAF fighter pilot, but the RAF insisted that he retire on medical grounds.

At the outbreak of World War Two, circumstances changed and he re-joined the RAF as a pilot, being credited with over 20 aerial victories during the Battle of France and the Battle of Britain. It was during the Battle of Britain that Douglas really showed off his skills as a pilot, openly displaying an aggressive attitude towards the German Third Reich. His courage and brashness were exactly what the RAF needed in their pilots in the early 1940's and as a result he was promoted to Wing Commander and given larger and larger formations of aircraft to lead. At the height of his wartime career in the RAF, Douglas was leading five Squadrons of fighters into Battle. This became known as the 'Big Wing' formation.

In August 1941 Douglas bailed out over German occupied France after colliding with another RAF fighter and he became a very reluctant Prisoner of War, despite being a double amputee. Douglas Bader bravely made numerous escape attempts and as a result was sent to Colditz Castle where he remained incarcerated until the end of the war. At one point the Germans confiscated his prosthetic legs to stop him from running away. Throughout his captivity, Wing Commander Douglas Bader remained a complete and utter pain in the arse for his Luftwaffe guards. During his incarceration, Douglas met and befriended one of the great German fighter aces of World War Two, the indomitable General Adolf Galland.

Adolf Galland

Adolf 'Dolfo' Galland was a German Luftwaffe General and flying ace who served in Europe throughout the Second World War. He flew over 700 combat missions and was credited with 104 aerial victories, seven of which were whilst flying a ME 262 jet fighter. His main choice of Luftwaffe aircraft was the Messerschmitt Bf 109 which he believed was superior to the Spitfire in the attack role, but he also thought the Spitfire was better defensively because although slower than the Bf 109, it was far more manoeuvrable.

During the Battle of Britain, Reichsmarschall Hermann Goering, the Head of the Luftwaffe, visited his units in France and remonstrated with them. Germany was losing too many bombers because they weren't being given effective fighter protection, Goering then asked his pilots what they needed to win the air battle over Britain. Major Werner Molders asked for more powerful engines to be fitted into their Bf 109's and Major Adolf Galland said to the Reichsmarschall, "I should like an outfit of Spitfires for my Squadron." Hermann Goering flew into a rage and stormed off. From that point on, the Reichsmarschall had it in for Adolf Galland. When Goering insulted his Luftwaffe fighter pilots' courage and skill, Galland vigorously defended them, which was a brave thing to as it could easily have cost him his life.

Adolf Galland and Douglas Bader were introduced after Bader was shot down in 1941 and met later on in the war whilst Douglas was a prisoner in Colditz Castle.

Colditz Castle - 1944

A German prison guard enters the cell where Douglas Bader is laid on his bed.

Guard: "Upstanden!"

Bader: "What's that, old boy?"

Guard: "Upstanden!"

Bader: "Listen Corporal, I haven't got a bloody clue what you're talking about!"

Guard: "Not Corporal - Feldwebel! Feldwebel is a Sergeant!"

Bader: "All right, Feldwebel, don't get your knickers in a twist. What is it you want?"

Guard: "You must stand to attention, Herr Bader! You have a very important visitor waiting to see you!"

Bader: "Oh, could you kindly inform Reichsmarschall Goering that I'm not receiving visitors today!"

Guard: " Ach, you English and your sense of humour! Your visitor is Herr General Galland!"

Bader: "Oh, General Galland. Just give me a moment will you and I'll get ready to see him."

Guard: "Nien! You must stand up now!"

Bader: "Look old chap, don't be so bloody thick! I have to strap my false legs on first. I'll only be a tick."

Guard: "Forgive me, of course. I will give you a moment then bring the General in."

Bader: "Before you leave, can I have some wood for the stove, old chum. We don't want the General getting a chill, do we?"

Guard: "I'll see what I can do for you, Herr Bader."

The Guard exits. He returns a short while afterwards carrying some kindling.

Guard: "This is all I could find, Herr Bader."

Bader: "Bloody Red Cross boxes eh! It would have been nice to have received some of the contents. Hope you enjoyed them."

Guard: "I received nothing, Herr Bader! That would be dishonourable, you will have to speak to the Herr Commandant about your Red Cross boxes. If you are ready, I will bring the General in."

Bader: "Crack on, old bean!"

The Guard exits. Bader continues strapping his false legs on.

Bader: "Bloody Krouts, think they own the place – which I suppose they do. No wonder they call this place Colditz – it'd freeze the balls off a brass monkey!"

He continues strapping his legs on, then stokes the small fire, trying to generate some heat from the feeble flames. The Guard enters, followed by General Adolf Galland.

Guard: "Upstanden! Schnell!"

Bader: "It may have escaped your attention you tit, but I'm still strapping my legs on!"

The General smiles as Bader finishes strapping his false legs on.

Galland: "Raus, Feldwebel!"

Guard: "Herr General!"

Guard salutes and exits the cell. General Galland shakes hands with Bader.

Galland: "My dear Douglas, how are you my friend?"

Bader: "Oh, I've been in better situations, Dolfie."

Galland: "I did warn you the last time that we met that you were pencilled in for the high security Oflag IV-C. We have to keep you Officers tucked away where it's safe."

Bader: "A right bloody dump this is. There's hardly any heating and the food's crap! Should be ashamed of yourselves! Can't wait to escape!"

Galland: "Not possible. Reichsmarschall Goering has declared that Oflag IV-C is escape proof!"

Bader: "What a load of old bollocks that is! The place leaks like a sieve!"

Galland: "Ha Ha. Here, I've brought you some chocolate, German I'm afraid and some coffee – Ersatz!"

Bader: "That's very kind of you, General. Come and sit by the stove, there's a lovely little fire going now."

Galland: "Ah, you have obtained some wood, Douglas."

Bader: "Yes, Red Cross boxes! Bugger all in them, just the boxes."

Galland: "Yes, I'm rather sorry about that."

Bader: "I'm sure that your bloody chaps in England get looked after better than we do here. It's disgraceful!"

Galland: "Fortunes of war, my dear fellow."

Bader: "'Suppose so. What are you doing in this neck of the woods, Dolfie? Have you come to surrender?"

Galland laughs.

Galland: "Hah hah, don't you wish, my friend! No, I flew in here for a meeting. It's one of the perks, having my own aircraft. Thought I'd call in and pay my respects."

Bader: "I should think so too! Perhaps next time you could bring me some cigarettes and maybe a bit of decent food. Some bacon and eggs would be nice."

Galland: "If there is a next time. I have some not very nice people snapping at my heels, Goering for one!!"

Bader: "Oh dear, that bad is it?"

Galland: "Afraid so. The Schweinhunds!"

Bader: "Can't you just have a word with old Schickelgruber; he must be a mate of yours?"

Galland: "Schickelgruber?"

Bader: "Your Fuhrer, you know, the bloke who chews carpets in Berlin."

Galland: "Douglas, you really need to be a little more careful. One never knows who is listening. Anyway, he doesn't actually chew carpets, no more than your Winston Churchill does!"

Bader: "Listen, I've got an idea. Why don't you sneak me out of here to your aircraft and we can both fly over to England. You'll be a prisoner but that won't be for too long the way things are going. The Yanks will be here shortly."

Galland: "That wouldn't be very honourable, now would it?"

Bader: "It's not very honourable you supporting the Nazis, is it?"

Galland: "I am not a Nazi supporter, Douglas, as you well know. I am, like you, a professional officer. I do my duty in the Luftwaffe as you do, or did, in the Royal Air Force."

Bader: "Keep your shirt on old boy, I didn't mean anything by it. My apologies if you're offended."

Galland: "Apology accepted. I'm not happy with what I have to do, but we must all obey our orders and do our duty, is that not so?"

Bader: "Suppose so. Well, my duty as an Officer is to escape from here."

Galland: "If you do, and you are re-captured then you will probably be shot. It is the way of things now."

Bader: "Don't worry, they won't catch me once I'm out of the main gate. I'll be back in England before you can say Heinrich Himmler! By the way, is it true that he's only got one ball?"

Galland: "Ah Douglas, you are incorrigible. Look at the time, I should go. I mustn't keep the Reichsfuhrer waiting."

Bader: "Ah, you're meeting up with old fatty Goering are you! Do give him my regards and tell him from me that his days are numbered. There's a silken rope waiting for his porky neck!"

Galland: "Ha Ha, I think not. I shall try and get back here to see you when I can. Until then, why not be a good boy and sit out the rest of the war quietly."

Bader: "Don't think so. Anyway, nice to see you again – oh, and thanks for the coffee and the chocolate."

Galland: "I'm sure you'll be bribing someone with it before the hour is out! Auf Wiedersehen my friend."

Galland laughs and they shake hands.

Bader: "Cheerio Dolfie, see you in London for a beer or two!"

Galland exits, still laughing. The Guard comes in.

Bader: "I say, Fritz, fancy a bit of chocolate?"

Guard: "My name is Helmut! Did you say Chocolate, Herr Bader?"

Bader: "Yes, chocolate. It's German crap I'm afraid – but beggars can't be choosers."

Guard: "Nicht werstehen! Er, I do not understand."

Bader: "Oh never mind, Helmut. Here, have a chunk!"

Guard: "Danke schoen, Herr Bader."

Bader: "Nice isn't it. Now, there's a little something I'd like you to get for me in exchange for that chocolate."

Guard: "And what is that?"

Bader: "A fully fuelled Spitfire!"

The Guard looks at Bader and they both burst out laughing.

<u>Footnote</u>: Terry Cavender was taking part in a military exercise in what was then West Germany, when a small group of Officers, including his Officer Commanding (OC) decided to call into a local hostelry for a drink and something decent to eat. At one end of the bar was sat a small, elderly and dapper German, all by himself. Terry and his comrades were carrying 9mm SMG's (Sub Machine Guns), which were obviously unloaded, and they tucked the weapons out of sight under a table. As they chatted amongst themselves whilst drinking a few beers, the German gentlemen came across to their table. He smiled and politely asked if he could examine one of the SMG's. Terry and the other soldiers rather sniffily replied, that they couldn't allow that, and so the old man bowed his head respectfully and returned to his own seat.

The owner of the pub sidled across to the group and said – "Meine Herren, may I respectfully point out to you that the man you have just been speaking with is Herr General Adolf Galland." He then swept off to recharge the British glasses. Of course, being of a certain age, the British knew who the General was. The OC went across to him, saluted and apologised for not treating him with the respect he deserved. Galland had been a 'proper' Officer and Gentleman – not one of the Nazi baddies! Naturally they allowed him to have a play with an SMG and spent about fifteen minutes just chatting with him about what they were up to that day. Adolf Galland was very pleasant and knowledgeable. Eventually Terry and the others had to leave the pub and returned to the rigours of their Exercise. Before leaving they went across to the General, saluted and bade him farewell. He just smiled and waved at them as they left.

2. LIEUTENANT COLONEL JOHNNY FROST

AND

MAJOR GENERAL ROY URQUHART

(ARNHEM – 1944)

Johnny Frost and Roy Urquhart

(Urquhart photo - Sergeant D M Smith, Army Film & Photographic Unit - Imperial War Museum Collection)

Lieutenant Colonel Johnny Frost was the son of a British Army Officer and was probably pre-destined for a career in the British Army. After joining up in 1932 he graduated from RMA Sandhurst, being commissioned as a Second Lieutenant into the Cameronians (Scottish Rifles). He served with the 'Jocks' until 1941 when a new and exciting challenge within the British Army tempted him away from his parent Battalion. Transferring into the newly formed Airborne Forces of the Parachute Regiment, by 1942 he had been promoted to Major and was tasked with leading C Company of 2 Para on 'OPERATION BITING!' With 120 paratroopers he had to dismantle and steal some important radar equipment from a German Army radar station near Bruneval in France. The successful raid resulted in three paratroopers being killed and seven badly injured, but they came back with the necessary 'borrowed' parts and also captured a German soldier who was an expert on the Luftwaffe's Radar equipment. Major Frost was awarded the Military Cross (MC) for leading the successful operation. He was eventually promoted to Lieutenant Colonel and commanded 2 Para through 'OPERATION TORCH' in Tunisia for which he was awarded a Distinguished Service Order (DSO), then 'OPERATION HUSKEY' in Sicily and part of the Italy campaign.

Johnny Frost is best known for commanding 2 Para in the Battle of Arnhem during 'OPERATION MARKET GARDEN'. 1st (British) Airborne Division was under the command of Major General Roy Urquhart, its total force amounted to nearly 10,000 paratroopers. They were tasked with capturing and holding both ends of the Arnhem Bridge for two to three days until being relieved by XXX Corps. 2 Para's Drop Zone was located six miles from the bridge and out of the whole of 1st Airborne Division only 2 Para made it to the northern end of the bridge at Arnhem. Johnny Frost was the only senior officer at the bridge, commanding 550 men of all ranks. These included airborne soldiers of the Royal Army Service Corps (RASC), Royal Engineers (RE) and Royal Army Medical Corps (RAMC). The whole of 1st (British) Airborne Division were supposed to hold the bridge at Arnhem for two to three days at most. XXX Corps, under the command of Major General Brian Horrocks, should have arrived at the bridge to relieve them, but German soldiers blocking XXX Corps' route fought with such tenacity that the rescue mission was a failure. The British soldiers held the bridge for over a week before having to surrender, purely and simply because their ammunition ran out. Communication problems meant that 2 Para couldn't get in touch with Roy Urquhart at his headquarters just a few miles away in Oosterbeek, to the West of Arnhem.

Whilst the main thrust from the South was taking place, Major General Roy Urquhart was trying to fight through the German troops that surrounded Johnny Frost at the bridge. The fighting was so intense that none of the other troops from 1st Airborne Division actually managed to link up with Johnny Frost. It was only through some freak weather conditions that Roy Urquhart eventually established radio communications with Johnny Frost at the bridge, some six days later.

Roy Urquhart: "Hello Johnny this is Roy. Over."

Johnny Frost: "Oh hello sir, nice of you to give me a call. Over."

Roy Urquhart: "Yeah sorry I've not been in touch, things have been a bit busy here in Oosterbeek. Over."

Johnny Frost: "I know what you mean sir, it's been quite hectic here as well. Over."

Roy Urquhart: "What's your situation Johnny? Over."

Johnny Frost: "Oh it's not too bad here sir. None of us have had much to eat for the last few days and we're running out of pretty much everything including water. We're getting pretty low on ammunition as well, which could prove a bit problematic. Other than that we're in pretty good shape considering. Over."

Roy Urquhart: "Oh dear, not getting any resupplies from the RAF? Over."

Johnny Frost: "No, not a sausage I'm afraid sir, in fact if the RAF did drop any sausages we'd have a hell of a punch up over who'd get to eat the damned things. Over."

Roy Urquhart: "Ha ha! Glad to hear you're keeping your sense of humour. What are you doing about the shortage of ammo?"

Johnny Frost: "Well sir, we've decided to take what we can off any dead Germans we come across and try to kill the rest of them using their own ammo. Seems only fair to give it back to them using their captured weapons. Over."

Roy Urquhart: "Good thinking Johnny, you always were an upright and honest officer and gentleman. Over."

Johnny Frost: "Any chance of you popping in at some stage sir? We were hoping you might come and rescue us, if you're not too busy. If you can't then I don't think we shall be able to hang on for very much longer. Some of my boys have resorted to strangling the enemy and throwing stones and insults. Jerry's starting to complain about some of the fruity language our paratroopers are using against them in their own dialect. Incidentally sir, can you tell me what a "Dorf arsch mampfen sohn aus ein prostituierte" is? Over."

Roy Urquhart: "I believe your chaps are calling the Germans "Stupid arse munching sons of prostitutes. Over."

Johnny Frost: "Oh dear, I'll have a word with the Adjutant about that and see if he can get them to stop it. I think it really is in bad taste, pardon the pun. Over."

Roy Urquhart: "Quite right Johnny, we don't want the Division getting a bad name. About rescuing you, I'm pretty sure we can't get through to the bridge, old chum. I'm really sorry but it appears you've been given the shitty end of the stick. Any chance you can make a break for it? Over."

Johnny Frost: "No chance, I'm afraid sir. We're totally surrounded, but the Krouts have yet to realise they are within a gnats nadger of losing this war. No matter how many of them we take out of the game they still keep coming back for more. Even if they weren't so aggressive I personally couldn't run for it, I've got shrapnel wounds in both of my feet. Over."

Roy Urquhart: "Sorry to hear that Johnny, looks like your heading for the bag. God bless you Johnny and good luck. It won't be for long though because this whole sorry war will be over soon. Monty and 'Boy' Browning are both optimistic that the Germans can't carry on for very much longer. Over."

Johnny Frost: "With respect sir, if those two believe that, then God help me and the rest of the British Army. Good luck Sir. Out!"

Lieutenant Colonel Johnny Frost surrendered to a senior German officer and was held as a prisoner of war at Spangenberg then later in a German hospital in Obermassfeldt. The US Army captured the hospital in March 1945 and freed Johnny Frost from his incarceration. For his leadership skills on the Bridge at Arnhem, Lieutenant Colonel Frost was awarded a Bar to his DSO. Before retiring from the Army in 1968 he attained the rank of Major General.

13. BRIGADIER MIKE CALVERT AND SERGEANT WILLIAM CLIFT (BURMA – 1944)

Brigadier Calvert
(Photo courtesy of the Imperial War Museum Collection)

Mike Calvert

Brigadier Mike Calvert was definitely an enigma in the true sense of the word, 'a person or thing that is mysterious or difficult to understand.' He was commissioned into the Royal Engineers in the early 1930's before serving in an RE Squadron in Hong Kong, but it was as a wartime soldier and commander that he really excelled and came to prominence. He personally witnessed the Japanese attack on China in 1937, which included the controversial 'Rape of Nanking.' It is believed that in just six weeks nearly 300,000 men, women and children of the Chinese nation were raped, tortured and murdered by the Japanese Army. After witnessing just some of these atrocities, Mike Calvert knew exactly what the British Army was going to face when fighting against the Japanese Armed Forces.

During the Second World War Mike Calvert saw action as a commando during the brief Norway campaign; he then trained other commandos in the art of 'blowing things up.' As a typical Royal Engineer he loved blowing things up more than he liked building things. Mike Calvert was then posted to Hong Kong and Australia were he continued to instruct soldiers in the art of destroying things with explosives. In 1941 he was put in command of a Bush Warfare Centre in Burma, where he taught Officers and NCO's about guerrilla operations. Some of his students eventually went to China and helped the Chinese nation in their fight against the Japanese Army.

The Japanese Army expanded their domination of the Far East by invading Burma. This, they hoped, would be the start of a Japanese campaign to overrun India where they'd filch the riches that the sub-continent had to offer. It was after the British Army retreated back to India from Burma that Mike Calvert met and worked with Major General Orde Wingate. Between them they formed some British guerrilla style units that Orde Wingate nick-named the Chindits. The name Chindits was a bastardisation from a mythical Burmese creature called a Chinthe. Ornate stone statues of these fictitious beasts can be seen 'guarding' Burmese temples and pagodas.   The clandestine Chindit troops operated deep behind enemy lines, blowing up railway tracks and proved to be a massive nuisance to the Japanese Army.   They operated on the same Lines as the Special Air Service did in the Middle East, whilst fighting Erwin Rommel's German Afrika Korps.   Orde Wingate and Mike Calvert planned two deep penetration raids behind the Japanese lines, 'OPERATION LONGCLOTH' and 'OPERATION THURSDAY.'

'OPERATION LONGCLOTH' was the first and smaller of the long range Operations behind Japanese lines. In 1943, Mike Calvert led over 3,000 Chindits and 1000 mules into Burma where his force caused mayhem amongst the Japanese army. Mike and his Chindits destroyed the Burma railway lines which was the main Japanese source of re-supplying their troops, the sabotage put the rail-tracks out of action for weeks. Extra Japanese troops had to be drafted in to cut off the supposed Chindits own supply lines, but the Japanese commanders soon realised that the Chindits were being re-supplied in the jungle by air (this was the first time air-despatching had been tried). The extra troops drawn off other Japanese Divisions had a detrimental effect on the Battle of Kohima, General Mutaguchi Renya stating, "The Chindit invasion...had a decisive effect on our Operations...one more Regiment would have turned the balance at the Battle of Kohima." Japanese Generals subsequently ordered their soldiers to cease being a blocking force and told them that they were to pursue the Chindits without prejudice. After four months of living and fighting behind enemy lines, Mike Calvert returned to India with about two thousand men who were in such a poor condition that only 600 of them were eventually fit enough to return back to active duty. He was awarded a Distinguished Service Order (DSO) for his part in 'OPERATION LONGCLOTH.'

'OPERATION THURSDAY' took place in 1944 and involved moving a much larger formation of approximately 10,000 soldiers, combining various regiments including artillery units, but this time they were all going to be flown into the Japanese held jungle. Soldiers were airlifted into Landing Zone Broadway, using American C 47 Douglas Dakota aircraft and Waco gliders and when fully established, they immediately started combating the Japanese. At one point Mike Calvert personally led a bayonet charge up Pagoda Hill to evict some Japanese soldiers from their entrenched position. He secured the ridge, his actions that day earning him the nickname, 'Mad Mike.' At the same time Lieutenant George Cairns of the Somerset Light Infantry won a Victoria Cross (VC) after having an arm chopped off by a Japanese Officer using a samurai sword. George killed the officer, picked up the sword and continued to charge towards the enemy, killing and wounding several other Japanese soldiers using just the captured weapon.   When 'OPERATION THURSDAY' was over,

Mike Calvert and his Chindits were flown back to India and he was awarded a Bar to his DSO. Orde Wingate was unfortunately killed in an air crash before the end of 'OPERATION THURSDAY.'

'Mad Mike' was flown back to England due to a medical problem and when fully recovered he was given Command of the Special Air Service (SAS) Brigade until it was disbanded in late 1945. Five years later he formed and led a unit called the Malayan Scouts who fought during the counter-insurgency campaign in Malaya. This formation resulted in the resurrection of the SAS Regiment that had been disbanded at the end of World War Two. During the campaign Brigadier Calvert again had to be medically evacuated, but this time it was because he was suffering from mental and physical exhaustion. Calvert reverted back to the rank of Lieutenant Colonel and was posted into a menial administrative job in an outpost called Soltau in North Germany. Because he was prone to bouts of alcoholism, Mike Calvert became very unpopular with his hierarchy. During the Second World War he was already unpopular with some Regular British Army Officers because of their general distrust and jealousy of all Special Forces, that, and because of the rumours that Brigadier Mike Calvert may have been gay. Up until 12th January 2000 being gay automatically precluded a person from serving in the British Armed Forces. The Army Act 1955 and its preceding laws considered homosexuality to be a military crime.

Gay servicemen have secretly served in the Armed Forces as far back as anyone would care to remember and some of those suspected have been our greatest warriors. Lieutenant Colonel 'Paddy' Blair Mayne SAS, Lawrence of Arabia and more recently the Paras in 3 Para Mortars Platoon are just some who were under suspicion. Like Mike, there wasn't any evidence to prove the accusations that they were actively practicing a gay lifestyle, but in the cases of 'Paddy' Mayne and Mike Calvert the rumours were enough to have an unfavourable effect. 'Paddy' was the most decorated soldier in World War Two, having won a total of four DSO's (second only to the VC) and he was also given a recommendation to be awarded a VC, but the rumours were enough to deny him Britain's top gallantry medal. Mike Calvert was also awarded two DSO's and when he led that bayonet charge on Pagoda Hill and cleared the Japanese held ridge, he really should have been awarded a VC, but again…those rumours.

During his posting to Soltau, Mike met some young German lads in a local pub called the Green Hunter, the lads were aged between 17 and twenty years old. They accused Mike of carrying out sexual acts of gross indecency on them in his flat and he was Court Martialled as a result. The Officers on the Court Martial board found him guilty and even after a post-trial investigation they refused to accept statements from the young lads saying that they had lied during the trial and that their evidence was false and misunderstood. The judge also refused to accept their statements because they weren't given to a Police Officer. The British Army turned its back on Mike Calvert and he was so devastated that his military career was ending in such a tragic and sordid fashion that he moved to Australia where he unsuccessfully attempted to resurrect an engineering career, mainly due to his alcohol addiction. Mike wrote several books and appeared on a documentary programme called 'The World at War' and he was a constant supporter of the Chindits Association. This superb and fearless Officer died in 1998, aged 85.

Sergeant William (Bill) Clift

Sergeant William Clift was born on 30th March 1919. After leaving school he worked in the mine at St Georges pit in the Tyldesley Colliery, near Bolton in Lancashire. In 1937 Bill joined the Territorial Army and served in the 5th Battalion of the Loyal (North Lancashire) Regiment for just over a year before joining the Regular Army as a Gunner in the Royal Artillery. Little is known about Bill's service career except that he ended up being posted out to the Far East. Come 1944 he was a Sergeant serving with the 1st Battalion South Staffordshire Regiment as part of Mike Calvert's 77th Indian Infantry Brigade.

On 31st March 1944, 3856262 Sergeant William Henry Clift was recommended for an award of the Military Medal (MM) for his actions on Henu Hill whilst part of the Chindit Force deployed on Operation Thursday. The citation read:

Throughout the actions on Henu on the 17th March 1944, this NCO showed great gallantry both in holding the positions under heavy fire and also in the attack on HENU HILL in the afternoon.

In the counter attack, he was always at the front throwing grenades and killing several enemy with his sten gun. When his platoon commander was killed, he rallied the platoon and still continued attacking until the position was captured. In this action, he personally attacked an officer killing him and capturing his sword. On March 23rd, again when the Platoon Commander was seriously wounded in the counter attack, again he assumed command and led his platoon.

In all these actions, this NCOs splendid example was an inspiration to his men.

Recommended by: Major R Degg OC 1st Battalion South Staffordshire Regiment and Brigadier J M Calvert DSO

Signed by: Major General W D A Lentaigne Commander 3rd Indian Division and General G Giffard Commander-in-Chief 11 Army Group

(London Gazette 27 July 1944)

One can only imagine the conversation between Brigadier Mike Calvert and the Lancastrian Sergeant Bill Clift after his citation was read out and he was presented with his MM in front of the Battalion.

Mike Calvert: "Congratulations Sergeant Clift and well done."

Bill Clift: "Mooch appreciated sir."

Mike Calvert: "I actually saw you in action on the 17th and backed up Major Degg's recommendation for this award. You displayed extraordinary courage Sergeant."

Bill Clift: "I were ownly dooin wor eye 'ad to dew sir, them blewdy Nips killed me boss and sum o' ma lads, I 'ad to stop the perishers sir."

Mike Calvert: "What was your job before you joined the army?"

Bill Clift: "I wor a Marner, you know, down t'pit, sir."

Mike Calvert: "A tough job, what."

Bill Clift: "It won't a patch on this bugger tho sir, believe me. I think ar'd rather be darn't t'pit. At least tuther Marners dowen't shoot at yer."

Mike Calvert: "Quite. Well, you've achieved something extraordinary, Sergeant. Because of your outstanding courage you probably saved many lives of the men in your platoon."

Bill Clift: "Ar dunt think ar deserve it reelly sir, ar mean, a lorra mar lads wor in theer doin' exactly wor ar wer dewin. I think somma them should've gorra a medal too sir."

Mike Calvert: "I think you are underestimating exactly what you've achieved Sergeant Clift. Your men only did what they did because they were inspired by your pluck and leadership."

Bill Clift: "Aye, mebee's sir but I still dun't think ar dun anything anyone else woodna dun…sir."

Mike Calvert: "You have made your mark in history Sergeant and your country will never forget that! You are a true hero."

Bill Clift: "Dun't know abahrt that sir. Ah, think me Mum and Dad'll be pretty chuffed tho. "

Mike Calvert: "I'm damned sure they will be, Sergeant."

Bill Clift: "Dew yer think we'll be gerrin 'ome soon sir?"

Mike Calvert: "I really couldn't say Sergeant, unfortunately I'm not a clairvoyant."

Bill Clift: "Are yew not sir?"

Mike Calvert: "Fraid not."

Bill Clift: "Sir, joost wor is an, er, clairvoyant?"

Mike Calvert: "Oh, it's a soothsayer, er, someone who predicts the future."

Bill Clift: "Ah, reyt, like you get a t'fairground. One o' them boogers."

Mike Calvert: "That's correct, so unfortunately I can't do it. If we could look into the future and see what was held in store for us, maybe we wouldn't do the things we do."

Bill Clift: "Aye, mebees yur right sir. Shall ar mek me whey back tew the platoon nar sir?"

Mike Calvert: "Yes, and again, jolly well done Sarn't Clift. We're all very proud of you."

14.   COLONEL PAUL TIBBETS AND CREW OF THE 'ENOLA GAY' (HIROSHIMA - 1945)

Paul Warfield Tibbets, Jr. (born 23 February 1915 - died 1 November 2007). He was best known as the pilot of the Enola Gay, the first aircraft to drop an atomic bomb in the history of modern warfare.   Tibbets selected a B29 bomber whose usual aircraft commander was on leave at the time re-naming it the 'Enola Gay' in honour of his Mother. The bomb, code-named 'Little Boy', was dropped on the Japanese city of Hiroshima, with horrendous consequences.

Tibbets was part of the USAF's 509th Composite Group that conducted the bombins of both Hiroshima and Nagasaki. At 0245 hours on 6th August 1945, the Enola Gay took off from Tinian airfield on the Mariana Islands with Colonel Paul Tibbets and Captain Bob Roberts at the controls. The Enola Gay's crew on that historic day consisted of 12 men:

Colonel Paul Tibbets– Pilot and Aircraft Commander.
Captain Robert Lewis – Co-pilot.
Major Thomas Ferebee – Bombardier.
Captain 'Dutch' Van Kirk– Navigator.
Captain William Parsons – Weaponeer and Mission Commander.
First Lieutenant Jacob Beser – Radar Countermeasures.
Second Lieutenant Morris Jepson – Assistant Weaponeer.
Technical Sergeant George 'Bob' Caron – Tail Gunner.
Technical Sergeant Wyatt E. Duzenbury – Flight Engineer.
Sergeant Joe S. Stiborik – Radar Operator.
Sergeant Robert H. Shumard – Assistant Flight Engineer.
Private First Class Richard H. Nelson – VHF Radio Operator.

As it was approximately 2,000 miles (3,200 km) away from Japan, it took six hours for the B29 bomber to reach Hiroshima. 'Little Boy' was dropped over Hiroshima at 0815 hours local time. Tibbets recalled that a tall mushroom cloud covered the city after the bomb detonated. He said afterwards, "I sleep clearly every night. I knew when I got the assignment that it was going to be an emotional thing. We had feelings, but we had to put them in the background. We knew it was going to kill people right and left, but my one driving interest was to do the best job I could so that we could end the killing as quickly as possible."

When Japan surrendered on 2nd September 1945, it finally brought the hostilities of the Second World War to a close.

ON BOARD THE ENOLA GAY

Lewis: "Colonel, excuse me Colonel."

Tibbets: "Oh, sorry, I must have dozed off for a few seconds there."

Lewis: "Not a problem sir. It's Zero Seven Forty-five hour's sir. We're approaching the target."

Tibbets: "Jeez, I'd welcome a slug of coffee before we get started."

Lewis: "No problem Colonel. Wyatt – you there?"

Duzenbury: "Sure am sir."

Lewis: "You got any hot Java left, Wyatt?"

Duzenbury: "Sure have Captain."

Lewis: "How about you bringing the Colonel a mug. Would you mind?"

Duzenbury: "My pleasure Captain. I'll just unplug and be right along."

Tibbets: "Thanks guys, you've made an old guy very happy. *(Tibbets touches his throat mike)* Lootenant Jepson! It's time to remove the safety devices on 'Big Boy', let's get it primed. Approximately thirty minutes to target boys."

Jepson: "I'm on it Colonel,"

Lewis: "Well, the old Enola Gay has done us proud so far. Six hours and not a blip from her engines."

Tibbets: "She sure is a good aircraft, Bob. Makes you feel sorta proud. Let's just keep our fingers crossed that 'Little Boy' does his job as well."

Technical Sergeant Duzenbury entered the cockpit carrying a mug of coffee for the Colonel.

Duzenbury: "Morning Colonel! Here's your coffee. Piping hot."

Tibbets: "Thanks Wyatt. Just what I need. Rest of the boys OK?"

Duzenbury: "Sure are Colonel. Fired up and ready to go!"

Jepson: "Colonel, the bomb's primed and good to go."

Tibbets: "Roger that, Morris."

Duzenbury passed the coffee to the Colonel.

Duzenbury: "Guess we're about to stir things up a little."

Lewis: "Only if the damn bomb does its job properly."

Tibbets: "I'm sure it will. They've spent enough man-hours working on it."

Duzenbury: "Hope that it make those Japs think twice about fighting on!"

Tibbets: "Well if it doesn't work we can always send in Errol Flynn to sort them out!"

They laugh.

Navigator: "Navigator to Pilot."

Tibbets: "Go ahead Theo."

Navigator: "Ten minutes to target, Colonel."

Tibbets: "Thanks. We good to go, guys?"

Ferebee: "Bomb doors open and confirmed good to go Colonel."

Parsons: "Yup, good to go Colonel."

Duzenbury: "I'll get back to my hell-hole, Colonel. Good luck sir!"

Tibbets: "OK everyone. Strap in and brace yourselves when the time comes. This 'ain't gonna be a pretty sight. Bob, if you could start the countdown with Tom then I'll give you the word when to let the bird fly."

Lewis: "You got it Colonel."

Ferebee: "Little Boy fully armed and ready to go sir."

Tibbets: "OK. Stand by everyone."

Mahiru Nakamuri is walking through the centre of Hiroshima, taking her son Baku to school. Baku's a bit grumpy because it's only a quarter past eight in the morning and he'd much rather be back at home in bed.

Mahiru: "Come Baku, get a move on or we'll be late and miss the bus again."

Baku: "But Mother, I'm so tired."

Mahiru: "Huh tired, indeed. How would it be if your Father said he was tired? He'd soon be in trouble with his officers!"

Baku: "But Father is a soldier, Mother. He has to be up early every day."

Mahiru: "Shush now Baku! What would our beloved Emperor think if he heard you talking like this?"

Baku: "Look, Mother, right up there. Something's shining in the sky. What is it?"

Mahiru: "Just the sun reflecting off an aircraft. They have very highly polished metal you know."

Baku: "Is it one of ours?"

Mahiru: "I'm sure it will be, my son."

Baku: "Yes, but what if it isn't?"

Mahiru: "Don't be afraid. We can come to no harm. Our beloved Emperor will protect us."

Baku: "Yes, but.."

Mahiru: "Come along now, Baku, time is short."

Meanwhile, back in the Enola Gay.

Tibbets: "Stand by. Everyone, make sure you've got your goggles on. OK, let it go!"

Ferebee: "Little Boy is on his way, sir."

Tibbets: "God help them down there."

Lewis: "Huh, they deserve everything that's coming to them!"

Tibbets: "OK, quiet please guys."

There is a flash followed by a tremendous explosion which throws the aircraft around in the sky. A huge mushroom cloud forms.

Lewis: "Jesus Christ! Will you just look at that!"

Tibbets: "Glad we're at this altitude, I wouldn't like to be too near that hell on earth. Guess we'd better head for home. This'll stir the Nip air force up a bit."

It was all very quiet in the aircraft and no-one spoke for a while.

Ferebee: "Looks like 'Little Boy' did the job on Hiroshima."

Lewis: "Yeah, guess so. You know Colonel, a lotta people must've died down there as a result of what we did today."

Tibbets: "Well whaddya expect, huh - there's a war on! We can't pussyfoot around with these people. Don't you think that they deserve it?"

Lewis: "It's just the women and children. I can't ..."

Tibbets: "We're not here to justify what we've just done. We're just obeying our orders and doing our job."

Lewis: "I know Colonel, but..."

Tibbets: "As I said, it's war. They started it, we're going to finish it. We'd better get used to this. I think that we'll be dropping a few more of these bombs until they get the message. They're very stubborn people the Japs."

Lewis: "Look at that cloud, it's like a huge mushroom. I'm never gonna forget this. It's scary."

Tibbets: "Yup, sure is. OK guys, job done. Let's head for home. There's gonna be a lotta questions want answering before we're much older, so make sure you write up your logs properly."

15. LIEUTENANT COLONEL JAMES CARNE
AND
A CHINESE OFFICER
(KOREA – 1951)

(Carne photo – Imperial War Museum collection)

Mention Korea today and it is likely that the name of the unhinged North Korean Dictator, Kim Jong-un, will spring to mind. There's a lot of history to all of this Korean business, but in essence, Kim Jong-un sees it as his destiny to re-unite North and South Korea, presumably under his leadership, and thereby become the leading force in his neck of the woods.

You would have thought that things would have quietened down a bit at the end of World War 2, but in 1950 the World very nearly descended into a Third, and nearly nuclear, World War. The battleground this time was on the 38th Parallel which was, and still is, the border of North and South Korea. Japan had ruled Korea from 1910 until the end of the Second World War, after which the country was divided up as the spoils of war between the United States and Russia. The Russians took control of everything north of the 38th parallel and the Americans governed everything to the south, however, trouble was bubbling under the surface between these differing Democratic and Communist Countries. Initially the split between North and South Korea was designed to be a temporary administrative solution but things got out of hand.

On 25th June 1950 over 75,000 soldiers of the North Korean People's Army invaded South Korea and started a war that continued from 1950 until 1953. As is usually the case with these things, the situation escalated under the leadership of the United States and the United Nations decided to join in, throwing their considerable weight behind the South Korean Government. The People's Republic of China decided to back the North Korean's because they wanted their neighbouring country to be communist ruled, at the same time the United States feared a communist world expansion. There are similarities, in principle, between that of Korea and West and East Germany. It could only end in tears and bloodshed and for three years that's precisely what happened.

The United Nations forces in South Korea consisted of troops from Australia, Belgium, Canada, Colombia, Ethiopia, France, Greece, India, Luxembourg, the Netherlands, New Zealand, the Philippines, South Africa, Thailand, Turkey and last, but not least, the United Kingdom. They all joined in military actions which it was stated were 'designed to prevent the conflict from spreading outside of Korea.' To cut a long story short, by July 1951 after a great deal of very bitter fighting, the conflict had reached a stalemate, with neither side being in a position to force the other's surrender. Eventually an armistice was declared but a lot of lives had been lost in between. Part of this scenario involved the heroic and gallant actions of Lieutenant Colonel James Carne of the Gloucester Regiment. He was not a politician, nor a man seeking power and position but a professional and very brave officer, serving in the finest traditions of the British Army.

Between the 22nd and 25th of April 1951, Lieutenant Colonel Carne and 750 members of the Gloucester Regiment fought over 10,000 North Korean and Chinese soldiers at Hill 253 on the Imjin River in Korea. When the 'Glorious Glosters' were finally given the order to break out, only 40 men managed to reach safety, the Chinese captured or killed the remainder. Lieutenant Colonel Carne was captured and imprisoned in North Korea and cruelly kept in solitary confinement where he was subjected to what was loosely termed, 're-education.' He was eventually released in September 1953 and returned home to England. The following month he was awarded the Victoria Cross (VC) for his gallantry and leadership at Hill 253 near the Imjin River.

We can only imagine the horrors of fighting in Korea, the appalling weather, the insects, the lack of water, medical supplies, ammunition and the seemingly insurmountable numbers of Chinese soldiers. We'd like to think that the following conversation might have taken place between the Colonel and his captors.

Chinese Officer: "Well, Colonel Carne, it seems that for you the fighting is at an end."

Carne: "It would appear so. I take it that you are an officer?"

Chinese Officer: "I am not here to answer your questions, Colonel! You are here to answer mine. But, yes, I am an officer and that is all you need to know. You are the vanquished, we are the victors. Your life and the lives of your men are now in my hands."

Carne: "How are my chaps, incidentally?"

Chinese Officer: "Don't concern yourself with your men, those few that remain. They will be well looked after, I can assure you."

Carne: "They had better be! You will be held responsible for them – all of them."

Chinese Officer: "Hah, responsible to whom? No-one knows that we have you and you don't even know who I am. I could give an order to have you executed and left here to rot. No-one would be any the wiser."

Carne: "Is that how you and your fellow officers behave?"

Chinese Officer: "As I said, I am not the one answering questions – you are! Cigarette?"

Carne: "No thank you. So, what happens now?"

Chinese Officer: "You will be taken from here to somewhere more appropriate and then will begin your re-education."

Carne: "Re-education? Now look here, my men and I are entitled to be treated properly, as Prisoners of War."

Chinese Officer: "Silence! Do not presume to lecture me about Prisoners of War. You are nothing at all. You are ours to do with as we wish. You can only help yourself by helping me."

Carne: "Do you mind if I say something?"

Chinese Officer: "Be my guest."

Carne: "I must compliment you on your English. It's really quite good."

Chinese Officer: "Oh, do you think so?"

Carne: Yes, not bad at all. University?

Chinese Officer: "If you must know, I was in London for a number of years, under cover, working in a restaurant. You English are so arrogant, you come into our restaurant's – which are everywhere by the way, and talk about anything. The information we collected over the years was invaluable, particularly from our places in central London."

Carne: "Ah that explains it then."
Chinese Officer: "Explains what?"

Carne: "Oh, I just detected a whiff of cockney in your accent."

Chinese Officer: "Really. Well of course we didn't all get the opportunity to have as polished an education as you English gentlemen, Colonel."

Carne: "One doesn't have to be educated in order to behave like a gentleman, does one? I mean, look at you for instance."

Chinese Officer: "We, the Chinese and our Korean brothers are fighting this war to get rid of 'Gentlemen' such as yourselves and have fairer, more balanced societies. You and people like you with your unearned privilege fill me with loathing. You just take anything that you want. It is unacceptable."

Carne: "Incidentally, could I have my watch back, please?"

Chinese Officer: "Your watch?"

Carne: "The one that you're wearing on your left wrist."

Chinese Officer: "Why? You don't need it. Time bears no importance for you anymore."

Carne: "Well, I'm feeling a bit peckish and I just wanted to know if its lunchtime. I presume that we're being getting fed, even though we're prisoners?"

Chinese Officer: "You and your men will receive the same rations as we do."

Carne: "Oh splendid – I'm rather partial to Chinese food. Er, my watch?"

Chinese Officer: "Here, you can have it. It will serve to remind you of better times!"

Carne: "Well old chap, neither of us is going to be here forever, are we? Who knows, maybe we can get together when all this unpleasantness is over and have a civilised meal somewhere nice, and a glass or two of chilled beer, eh?"

Chinese Officer: "Ah, the English. To you everything is a joke."

Carne: "Well old boy, one has to make the best of a bad thing. I'm sure that you'll find that out in due course once you're in the cage!"

Chinese Officer: "I'm sure that I won't, old boy."

Carne: "Listen, let's be reasonable. I'm happy to chat with you all day, but for starters I'd like to know with whom I'm speaking. My name, as I'm sure you know, is James Carne, and you are?"

Chinese Officer: "I don't suppose it will do any harm you knowing my name. I am known as Mao Tse-Tung."

Carne: "Oh right. Mao Tse-tung. Bit of a mouthful, that. I suppose a cup of tea and a biscuit's out of the question, Mao?"

Chinese Officer: "You will be punished for your insolence! GUARD!!"

16. WO1 (RSM) RONALD BRITTAIN
(ROYAL MILITARY ACADAMY SANDHURST – 1954)

(Drawing courtesy of Nicky Clacy)

What is a Warrant Officer Class 1 (Regimental Sergeant Major) - (WO1 (RSM))? Well, there are many and varied opinions about this question, with answers ranging from an RSM being the absolute epitome of professionalism in the non-commissioned ranks of the British Army, down to being the 'Son of Satan.'

Warrant Officers were first introduced into the British Army on the 1st January 1879. A class of Warrant Officers was constituted, 'to assist in the discharge of the subordinate duties of the Commissariat and Transport and of the Ordnance Store Departments of our Army, to be denominated 'Conductors of Supplies' and 'Conductors of Stores' respectively.

In essence, Regimental Sergeant Major (RSM) is an appointment held by Warrant Officers Class 1 (WO1) in the British Army, the British Royal Marines and in the armies of many Commonwealth and former Commonwealth nations, including Ireland, Australia and New Zealand; and by Chief Warrant Officers (CWO) in the Canadian Forces. Only one WO1/CWO holds the appointment of RSM in a regiment or battalion, making him the senior warrant officer. In a unit with more than one WO1, the RSM is considered to be "first amongst equals." The RSM is primarily responsible for maintaining standards and discipline and acts as a parental figure to his or her subordinates and also to junior officers, even though they, 'technically', outrank him.

Probably the most famous and revered such individual was the late RSM Ronald Brittain of the Coldstream Guards, born 12th September 1899 – died 9th January 1981, famed throughout the land and remembered by all those who crossed paths with him. He was deemed to have had the loudest voice ever in the British Army and was definitely not to be tangled with. Rumour had it that he even had his badge of rank sewn onto his pyjamas:

WO1 - Badge of Rank

and referred to his wife as "Corporal." He was an RSM of the old school who would probably not be tolerated in these days of political correctness. Notwithstanding, he put steel into many a spine when required to do so.

Imagine one gloomy day in the mid-1950's on the main parade square at the Royal Military Academy, Sandhurst where RSM Brittain is perambulating across the square in an orderly fashion, when he espies a couple of Arab gentlemen wandering around like lost souls. He is gobsmacked by their impertinence.

(RMA SANDHURST 1954)

RSM: "You two! Get your misbegotten lardy arses over here **NOW!** On the double you 'orrible little creatures!"

The two robed Arab gentlemen trot across the square and stand quivering in front of the RSM.

RSM: "Maaaaaark time on the spot! "Get those knees shoulder high!"

Arab 1: "Sir, Might I explain...."

RSM: "Stand still! Get your bleeding heels together and pull those shoulders back. You're like a twisted crisp! You don't want people thinking that you dance from the other side of the ballroom now, do you lads?!"

Arab 1: "Indeed not, sir."

RSM: "Don't address me as sir – I am not a commissioned officer – I am a Regimental Sergeant Major! Are you trying to demote me?"

Arab 1: "My apologies, Regimental Sergeant Major."

RSM: "Be quiet when you're speaking to me, you pond life!"

Arab 1: "Yes sir, er, Regimental Sergeant Major."

RSM: "Now then lad, what are you doing poncing around on my square wrapped in bed sheets and wearing that curvy sword thing, eh? You been to a fancy dress party?"

Arab 1: "Forgive me, but this is my national dress and the curvy sword is in fact a ceremonial scimitar."

RSM: "Well you look like a nonce – and who's that lurking behind you, Ali bleedin' Baba?"

Arab 1: "He is Ayeeb, my bodyguard."

RSM: "Your bleedin' bodyguard! This is Sandhurst, you don't need a bodyguard here. The only person you have to be afraid of is me! Is that clear?"

Arab 1: "Oh, I wouldn't question that for one moment Regimental Sergeant Major."

RSM: "You taking the piss, lad?"

Arab 1: "Certainly not."

RSM: "What's your name?"

Arab 2: "He is His Royal Highness Prince Abdullah Shamily bin Tak-Tak.

Arab 1: "I am here..."

RSM: "I didn't ask for your fuckin' life story, my lad! I just wandered why you two were, meandering, I said meandering - nay mincing - across my square as if you were on a fuckin' Sunday afternoon stroll?"

Arab 1: "Please allow me to explain..."

RSM: "**QUIET!** There's a parade due to march on here at any minute and I don't want you two vagabonds getting in the way! You see this pace-stick, well if you two don't get out of my sight within the next ten seconds then I will insert it where the sun don't shine. Are you with me?"

Arab 1: "But...."

RSM: "Shut your cake-hole, shrimp! Oh bloody hell, here's the Commandant. Now we're all in deep shit!"

Enter the Commandant. The RSM fires off a snappy salute.

RSM: "Morning Sir!"

General: "Everything tickety-boo, Mr Brittain?"

RSM: "Ah, just sorting out a little problem here, sir."

General: "Yes, I saw you from my office. Ah Mr Brittain, perhaps I should explain."

RSM: "No need for explanations, General. I found these two scruffy little shite-hawks strolling, would you believe it, strolling across the square as if they haven't got a care in the world. And I'm not really sure, sir, but when the wind blew this one's 'robe' up I could have sworn that he was wearing the devils cloth underneath!"

General: "The devils cloth, RSM?"

RSM: "Jeans sah! Bloody denim! Whatever next, eh! I'm just going to direct them to the Guardroom for a spot of enlightenment from the Provost Sergeant, sir. I think they're foreign students."

General: "RSM, if I may. As you are no doubt aware, today is the Sovereign's Parade."

RSM: "With respect sir, I didn't come to Sandhurst on a banana boat! I am fully aware of that sir, of course."

General: "Indeed. Well I'm sure that you are also aware that Her Majesty cannot be with us today and she has kindly nominated someone to attend in her stead."

RSM: "That's right sir, some Johnny foreigner I believe, sir?"

General: "Johnny foreigner, I say, that will never do RSM. Her Majesty has in fact invited His Royal Highness Prince Abdullah Shamily bin Tak-Tak to do her the honour of inspecting the parade and to take the salute on the march-past."

RSM: "Oh, you don't mean that this 'gentleman' here is ...."

General: "Yes I do, RSM. Your Royal Highness, may I introduce you to Regimental Sergeant Major Brittain."

Arab 1: "Oh Mr Brittain, I cannot tell you what a pleasure it has been to receive a bollocking from you. Quite memorable."

RSM: "My pleasure sir. No offence intended. You know, in one ear – out of the other."

Arab 1: "No offence taken, I assure you. I rather enjoyed it. I'm afraid that my bodyguard is shaking in his boots though."

RSM Brittain points his pace stick at Arab 2.

RSM: "Brace yourself, lad!"

General: "Might I suggest, your Highness, that we cut along to my office. I can introduce you to some of the other VIP guests and perhaps we could have a drop of something appropriate before the parade."

Arab 1: "Spiffing idea, General. Are you joining us, Mr Brittain?"

RSM: "Oh. No, no, no, sir. I've got to check that everything is tickety boo for the parade. You toddle off and enjoy yourself, sir."

General: "Er, this way your Highness."

The General, the Prince and his Bodyguard start to walk off the square.

RSM: Get in step, Gentlemen! Left, right, left, right .... *(Aside)* Bloody Ruperts!"

17. GRAND ADMIRAL DONITZ AND HIS PRISON COMMANDANT
(SPANDAU PRISON, WEST BERLIN – 1954)

(Dönitz photo – courtesy Bundes Arciv)

Grand Admiral Karl Dönitz joined the German Imperial Navy in 1911, transferring into its Submarine Service when it was founded. By the closing stages of the First World War he'd been promoted to Commander of the submarine UB 68. When it was sunk by the Royal Navy, he was taken prisoner on the Island of Malta, thirty eight days before the end of the war. He was then taken to England where he was held in a Prisoner Of War camp near Sheffield in Yorkshire until 1920. Continuing with his naval career after returning to Germany, in 1935 he rose to the rank of Kapitan zur See after being placed in command of a flotilla of submarines. In that same year the Reichsmarine, (German Navy), was replaced by the Kriegsmarine, (Nazi German Navy). During the Second World War his son Peter died whilst serving in a Kriegsmarine submarine. His other son, Klaus, was taken off active duty after the death of his brother; he was killed on his twenty fourth birthday whilst on a torpedo boat that was taking part in a raid.

Adolf Hitler committed suicide in April of 1945, whereupon Grand Admiral Karl Donitz was handed the unenviable task of being in charge of a destroyed Germany. He didn't want the job, blaming Albert Speer (the German Minister for Armaments and War Production from 1942 to 1945) for telling Adolf Hitler that Donitz should be his successor as Head of State. Speer denied this claim.

At the Nuremburg Trials, Dönitz was indicted for war crimes for which he refused to accept any responsibility. He also denied any knowledge of the Holocaust, even though in 1944 he had declared, "I would rather eat dirt than see my grandchildren grow up in the filthy, poisonous atmosphere of Jewry." On 18th July 1947 Dönitz was found guilty of war crimes and was transported from Nuremburg to Spandau Prison in West Berlin. Dönitz never showed any contrition for the actions he took during the war. He was sentenced to ten years imprisonment, during which time he only associated with one other prisoner, Erich Raeder who had commanded the surface Kriegsmarine. Bizarrely, even though they occasionally and briefly conversed with each other in Spandau prison, the pair of them held each other in total contempt.

On release from Spandau prison in September 1956, Dönitz made a brief attempt to enter German politics, but failed. He was particularly contemptuous of his Navy pension which was only granted to him at the rank level of Kapitan. The pension office stated that any other rank he gained in World War Two was achieved only at the largesse of Adolf Hitler. On his release from Spandau Prison, Dönitz retired to a small village just outside Hamburg, eventually dying there of a heart attack on 24th December 1980.

Spandau Prison

Spandau Prison was built in 1876 and was demolished in 1987 after Rudolf Hess, its last detainee, had died there under suspicious circumstances, reported to have been suicide. At the end of World War Two the prison held only seven inmates who had all been convicted at the Nuremburg War Trials. Each of the allied powers, Britain, France, the United States and Russia took it in turns to control and administer the prison. These duties were carried out consecutively for one calendar month by soldiers from each participating country and a formal, official handover/takeover was always carried out. In 1956 one of the Prison Commandants was Lieutenant Colonel Speirs who had served alongside Major Dick Winters in Easy Company 101st Airborne Division (Band of Brothers). The only British claim to fame comes from the fact that the comedian, the late Bernard Manning, was also a guard at the prison. Manning, being of a Russian/Jewish descent may have caused some irritation amongst those in his custody.

The Russian's insisted they would continue with these duties as long as any of the prisoners were still alive in Spandau Prison. They used it as an excuse to enter West Berlin (The Allied Sector) during the Cold War so they could monitor what the Western Forces were doing. The Nazi prisoners hated it when the Russians took over their stint because they were subject to more severe conditions. Food given to the prisoners whilst the Russian cooks were in charge of the cookhouse was particularly poor. The Western Powers were slightly concerned that if the last prisoner (Rudolf Hess) died whist the Russians were in control of the prison, they might not hand it back and they would then have a toe-hold in West Berlin.

Fortunately for us, Hess died whilst the British were in control of the prison and so the problem was averted. One wonders what the conversation between the Prison Commandant and Dönitz would have been like when he was released in 1956.

Prison Commandant: "Please take a seat, Herr Dönitz."

Dönitz: "I would rather stand, if you don't mind, Herr Commandant."

Prison Commandant: "As you wish. So you're leaving us today then, Herr Donitz. Fancy a drop of celebratory grog before you go old chap? I suppose the sun must be over the yard-arm somewhere in the world."

Dönitz: "Not for me, danke, Herr Commandant."

Prison Commandant: "Oh, now come on old boy, don't be bitter. It's all over now and someone has to win, what! Here, have a tot."

Dönitz: "Easy for you to say, Herr Commandant. I have been stripped of all my honours and awards, been confined to prison for ten years – and despite everything my government will only permit me to draw the pension of a mere Naval Captain! I was the Head of State for God's sake!"

Prison Commandant: "Steady on old bean! You win some, you lose some! There but for the grace of God and all that."

Dönitz: "To the victor the spoils eh. You know what Colonel, I think I will join you in a drink if I may."

Prison Commandant: "Good man. That's the spirit! 'Stand fast the Holy Ghost!' Here, let me pour one for you."

The Commandant pours Dönitz a glass of Lambs Navy Rum.

Prison Commandant: "As they say in our Royal Navy, 'Splice the Mainbrace!' Ah you can't whack it – Rum, Bum and Baccy!"

Dönitz: "I beg your pardon? I am not familiar with that phrase?"

Prison Commandant: "Oh it's just a saying that our Navy chaps use. Bottoms up! That's a phrase we use in the British Army!"

Dönitz: "Prost!"

Prison Commandant: "The Queen – God Bless her!"

Dönitz: "To Her Majesty."

They stand to attention and as they knock their rum back, Dönitz clicks his heels together.
Prison Commandant: "Oh – none of that heel clicking, Herr Dönitz. Not the done thing any more, old chum."

Dönitz: "My apologies. Old habits die hard."

Prison Commandant: "As the Priest said to the Nun, eh! Come on chum, lighten up a bit."

Dönitz: "Forgive me Colonel, but I find your British sense of humour difficult to comprehend."

Prison Commandant: "So what's going to happen to you now?"

Dönitz: "For me – there is nothing. I will return to my village in Aumhule and gently fade away."

Prison Commandant: "We've all got to drop anchor at sometime, more's the pity. Aumhule – where's that?"

Dönitz: "Just outside of Hamburg."

Prison Commandant: "Ah Hamburg. I'll bet you had some fine times there when you were a young whipper-snapper, eh!"

Dönitz: "Oh, I had my moments. And what will you do with yourself, now that the war is over, will you be a prison commandant for the rest of your career?"

Prison Commandant: "Oh, don't worry about me old boy. There's lots more for me to do; I'm only half way through my voyage."

Dönitz: "You have already achieved much in your life, you are a Colonel no less. I'll bet that they don't tinker with your pension!"

Prison Commandant: "Never say die old boy, that's me. It'll probably take a firing squad to get rid of me."

Dönitz: "Had things turned out somewhat differently I could probably have helped you with that!"

Prison Commandant: "Ha Ha – I see that you do have a sense of humour! Another sippers?"

Dönitz: "Ja, undt why not. We are only young once, as they say."
Copious amounts of Lambs Navy Rum are consumed by both of them.

Dönitz: "You know Colonel, if we'd had a supply of this rum for my fellows then I think things might have been different – we might have won!"

Prison Commandant: "I think it would've taken more than a few bottles of Lambs Navy Rum to do that old boy!"

Dönitz: "If only the Fuhrer had listened to what we were telling him then things would certainly have been different. You know, he was surrounded by grovelling sycophants, right up until the end. Scheisse!"

Prison Commandant: "Know just what you mean. It's the same with our politicians. Scheisse indeed, old bean. Er, noch ein?"

Dönitz: "Danke. Do you know, towards the end, that shifty little pig dog Himmler came limping into my Headquarters, as if he owned the place. I gave him short shrift!"

Prison Commandant: "What was he after?"

Dönitz: "He wanted to be Head of State would you believe! I told him that he could have the job as far as I was concerned, but that imbecile Albert Speer convinced the Fuhrer to appoint me as Head of State, verdammt! Himmler then had the audacity to ask me to appoint him as my Deputy! I showed him a copy of the Fuhrers last will and testament and told him to fuck off out of my headquarters. He turned as white as a sheet then slunk off into the night. Damned chicken farmer!"

Prison Commandant: "Well, we very nearly had him you know. Just couldn't get to him in time when he bit into his cyanide capsule. He managed to escape the hangman's rope."

Dönitz: "The same as fatty Goering. What a pair of comedians they were. Our own version of Laurel and Hardy."

Prison Commandant: "Comedians or not – they climbed to the top of a very shitty pile."

Dönitz: "As did I – but I did so, honourably. Undt what was my reward – ten years in prison. Me – Grand Admiral Karl Doenitz, a common prisoner! And now I am to be cast aside as some inconsequential side note in history."

Prison Commandant: "Well you've done your porridge now, old boy. Why not just toddle off back to your village, write a couple of books, sit back and enjoy yourself."

Dönitz: "One of your television crews has already been touch, actually. They are to film a series called "World at War" I think they said it was."

Prison Commandant: "Oh yes, I know about that, sounds jolly interesting. You should do it. There'll be a few Deutschmarks in it for you."

Dönitz: "Maybe I will. I still know where most of the skeletons are buried!"

Prison Commandant: "So do we all, old boy, so do we all! Cheers!"

Dönitz: "Prost! This rum is sliding down as easily as my U-Boats did in the Atlantic!"

Prison Commandant: "Yes, trouble is they never re-surfaced though! Prost!"

Dönitz: "Alas, many brave men were lost – on both sides. Prost!"

There is a tap on the door and the Commandant's CSM (Company Sergeant Major) walks in to inform the Commandant that there's a problem.

Prison Commandant: "Well Herr Dönitz, I suppose that it's time for you to step out into the big bad world as a free man. You'll find that it's not as bad as when you were in charge though."

Dönitz: "Jawhoul Colonel, oh - und may I say danke schön!"

Prison Commandant: "For what, old boy?

Dönitz: "For not treating me like the Russians did! They are barbarians!"

Prison Commandant: "Well, I suppose that they do see things rather differently."

The CSM coughs politely.

Prison Commandant: "What is it, Sarn't Major?"

CSM: "Er, spot of disquiet down in the cell block, sir."

Prison Commandant: "Buggeration, now what?"

CSM: "It's that bloody comedian Private Manning again sir. He keeps winding that git Rudolph Hess up with the joke about, 'Two Nazi's walk into a gay bar."

Prison Commandant: "And?"

CSM: "He won't tell him the punch-line!"

Prison Commandant: "Tell Manning to come and see me, immediately – I haven't heard that one!"

18. GENERAL DOUGLAS MACARTHUR
AND
LIEUTENANT WILLIAM CALLEY
(UNITED STATES OF AMERICA - 1969)

(Photo courtesy of the US Army Signal Corps Collection – US National Archive)

General MacArthur

General Douglas MacArthur (born on the 26th January 1880 - died on the 5th April 1964). An American Five Star General, MacArthur eventually became Field Marshal of the Philippine Army and Chief of Staff of the United States Army in 1937. McArthur was recommended for the Medal of Honour (the United States version of the Victoria Cross) after taking part in the Veracruz expedition in Mexico and when he fought in France during the First World War. He was turned down on both occasions, bitterly disappointing him because his father has previously won 'the big medal' during the American Civil War. He was also America's most decorated soldier in the Great War after winning two Distinguished Service Crosses, a Distinguished Service Medal, seven Silver Crosses, two Purple Hearts, and three French decorations for bravery. McArthur did eventually win a Medal of Honour for his role in the defence of the Philippines during World War 2. He also added two Distinguished Service Crosses to his amazing tally of gongs.

On the 2nd of September 1945 General McArthur accepted the Japanese surrender aboard the USS Missouri anchored in Tokyo Bay, he then oversaw the occupation of Japan from 1945 to 1951. It was during this period that the North Korean Army crossed the 38th Parallel which divided North and South Korea. After invading the US controlled country, they pushed the US Army all the way back to the Pusan perimeter. Douglas MacArthur commanded the mission to drive the communists back over the border at a time when certain defeat beckoned. He devised a brilliant seaborne invasion at Inchon, well behind enemy lines and forced the communist's back to the 38th Parallel. The communists were pushed back to the very north of North Korea and it was at that stage that MacArthur decided he wanted to push on into China. During the winter of 1950, US troops were again forced to retreat by a mixture of North Korean and Chinese soldiers and ended up back at the 38th Parallel. MacArthur discussed using nuclear weapons on Manchuria and Russia. His enthusiasm had to be curbed and so he was removed from the Korean War command by President Harry Truman on the 11th of April 1951. On return to the United States, General Douglas MacArthur gave a public speech in which he said "Old soldiers never die; they just fade away." He left the army shortly after giving that speech.

Lieutenant Calley

William Laws Calley is a former United States Army Lieutenant who served in South Vietnam in 1968. He was Court Martialled for murdering twenty two unarmed South Vietnamese civilians in the My Lai Massacre. One of four platoon commanders from C Company 1st Battalion 20th Infantry Regiment who took part in Operation Muscatine A O, a 'Search and Destroy' Operation. They were ordered to clear several Hamlets of all Viet Cong suspects, My Lai was Calley's particular area of operation. He and his platoon were flown by Huey helicopters into their LZ (Landing Zone) right next to the village. At the briefing, his superior, Captain Medina, allegedly gave unclear orders and some of the officers understood that anyone still in the village were Viet Cong or North Vietnamese Army. Medina is quoted as saying, "They're all VC now go and get them, destroy everything in the village that is walking, crawling or growing." Calley was also ordered to poison any wells they found. During the operation up to five hundred old men, women, children and babies were slaughtered in the ensuing one sided violence. Women were raped before being executed and victims were thrown down wells, hand grenades thrown in after them. Calley is alleged to have been personally responsible for twenty two of the deaths. Not all the soldiers on this operation joined in with the killing, Private First Class Carter shot himself in the foot so he could be evacuated and escape the madness.

Warrant Officer Hugh Thompson was flying his Huey helicopter over My Lai village and saw the mass of badly injured and dead civilians. After landing to see if he could help, he witnessed several atrocities but during the operation he managed to evacuate and save at least ten Vietnamese lives. Warrant Officer Thompson kept pushing for the soldiers in My Lai to be brought to justice and a Court Martial was convened two years later back in the United States, only Lieutenant Calley was found guilty of any war crimes. He was placed under house arrest for three years. President Nixon then reduced his sentence by virtue of a Presidential Pardon.

Lieutenant Calley suffered with Post Traumatic Stress Disorder (PTSD) after returning from Vietnam and also suffered from horrendous nightmares. One wonders how his dreams might have manifested themselves if General MacArthur visited him in his sleep.

MacArthur: "Ah Mister Calley, I've been wanting to meet you for quite some time."

Calley: "General, I am honoured to meet you, sir."

MacArthur: "Relax, take a seat, son. I'd just like to have a little chat with you, off the record..."

Calley: "I take it you want to talk to me about the Mai Lai massacre, General?

MacArthur: "That's correct son, but what I'm really interested in is how a professional commissioned officer who has received the best training in the best damned Army in the world took such an, how shall we say, 'unusual' course of action as you did at Mai Lai. Naturally I've read all of the official reports, but there's nothing like first-hand information."

Calley: "President Nixon didn't consider it 'unusual', sir. He knew that I was just doing my duty, and that in truth I was just a fall-guy for all of the bad stuff that was going down at the time. That's why I got a Presidential Pardon."

MacArthur: "Yup, I realise that Mr Calley, but we've all been in hellish spots. I mean look at me, I even had to kiss the Emperor of Japan's ass more than once! He was no different to Adolf Hitler."

Calley: "Yes, I have read about that sir, but it's not quite in the same league as Mai Lai, is it?"

MacArthur: "What I'm really trying to find out is if the end justifies the means."

Calley: "Frankly sir, I considered that I was just doing my duty."

MacArthur: "You can't really expect me to believe that now can you?"

Calley: "Sir, you had to be there. In the heat of battle, as you know, things can look very different, especially in that God-forsaken place, Vietnam."

MacArthur: "Agreed. OK, let's back-track a little here. Why not just tell me your side of the story."

Calley: "Sir, it was on the 16th of March 1968. I was on a Search and Destroy operation and led 1st Platoon, C Company, 1st Battalion, 20th Infantry Regiment, we arrived at 'Son My' village in helicopters."

MacArthur: "Yup, I know all about that routine stuff. Explain to me, briefly, why it was alleged that as well as the killings of men, women and children, which I accept are accidents of war, there was gang-rape and deliberate mutilation. You were also poisoning wells, I believe?"

Calley: "General, as you say sir, these things happen in wartime. On that particular day I couldn't be everywhere at once. Some of the men went far too far but what was done was done. It was truly hell on earth."

MacArthur: "But you as their Platoon Commander should have stopped anything untoward happening. Why didn't you step up to the plate, son?"

Calley: "As I said sir, I couldn't be everywhere at any one time. A lot of the really bad stuff had been done by the time I found out about it."

MacArthur: "The record states that between 347 and 504 unarmed civilians were slaughtered. You must have known, must have seen some of what was going on there?"

Calley: "Sir, I did see some of what was going on. What could I do, it was a nightmare. As the senior man there ultimately I was held responsible. That doesn't mean that I agreed with what happened. It just happened."

MacArthur: "You were convicted of taking out 22 of the villagers yourself weren't you, Mr Calley? Aren't you even just a little bit ashamed of that?"

Calley: "In the cold light of day it's easy for anyone to say that and just as easy for anyone who wasn't there to pass judgement on my actions."

MacArthur: "You were court martialled, fairly I believe, found guilty as charged and then handed a life sentence."

Calley: "That is correct sir. By the same token, I eventually received a Presidential Pardon."

MacArthur: "I'm trying to get my head around the whole scenario. I just wonder what I would have done had I been in a similar situation. It was referred to as the most shocking episode of the Vietnam War."

Calley: "With respect sir, just how do you think you would have reacted had you been in my position, with my level of seniority? I was just a Lieutenant?"

MacArthur: "I'd like to think that I would have behaved properly throughout, but who can tell. None of us really knows how we will behave when were out there doing a job that no-one in their right mind wants to do. I suppose that the only good thing to come out of it was that the American public were so outraged and disgusted that the Vietnam War was shortened. In a roundabout way that it saved many lives."

Calley: "Three of the guys there tried to stop what was going down in Mai Lai and look what happened to them – they were denounced as traitors! Where's the logic in that? It took some thirty years before they were recognized and decorated for their actions. As I said, I eventually received a Presidential Pardon. The President and his Advisors must have understood what happened to me and the others. How do you explain that?"

MacArthur: "Well, we all know that soldiering isn't just fine uniforms, bullshit and brass bands. When the crap hits the fan we all get splattered!"

Calley: "With respect General, usually at your level you're tucked away in some safe bunker, drinking coffee and calculating the butcher's bill!"

MacArthur: Easy son! I haven't always been a General and I didn't get there overnight you know! In World War 1, I was nominated for a Medal of Honour, awarded the Distinguished Service Cross twice and the Silver Star seven times. You don't get that for sitting on your butt in a safe place. I know what it's like to be in the thick of it."

Calley: "My apologies sir. I was not calling your bravery or honour into question, just the circumstances in which we find ourselves and how things work out. Had things gone differently for me I could have had plenty of medals and perhaps a successful military career."

MacArthur: "What, you mean like Audie Murphy?" (*)

(*) Footnote: Audie Leon Murphy (born 20th June 1925 – died 28th May 1971) was one of the most decorated American combat soldiers of World War 2, receiving every military combat award for valour available from the US Army,

as well as French and Belgian awards for heroism. 19-year-old Murphy received the Medal of Honour after single-handedly holding off an entire company of German soldiers for an hour at the Colmar Pocket in France in January 1945, then leading a successful counterattack while wounded and out of ammunition.

Calley: "Who can say General? It's often down to whatever fate decrees."

MacArthur: "I suppose that the passage of time will inevitably change how we assess things. Look at how the story of General Custer and the Battle of Little Big Horn has changed over the years. General Custer's now the bad guy!"

Calley: "That's my point sir. You do what you consider to be your duty at the time. Historical consequences figure at the bottom of your list of your priorities, when the lead's flying, General."

MacArthur: "I get all that, son, but don't we always have that little voice in the corner in our brain telling us just what's right and what's wrong."

Calley: "I can't deny that, sir."

MacArthur: "What happened to your little voice, your conscience?"

Calley: "I truly did what I thought was right at the time, sir. Guess you just had to be there."

MacArthur: "Had I been there, son, it probably wouldn't have happened."

Calley: "With respect, sir, that's just supposition!"

MacArthur: "I'd like you to call back here tomorrow night Mr Calley. We can continue to talk this through, if that's OK with you?"

Calley: "Yes General. I have nothing to hide, I just want to get these images out of my head."

MacArthur: "OK, I'll see you at the same time tomorrow night Mr Calley. You're dismissed!"

Calley: "Sir."

19. SERGEANT CLARKE RM AND TENIENTE COLOCCINI
(SOUTH GEORGIA - 1982)

The Santé Fe Submarine

Sergeant 'Nobby' Clarke RM and Teniente De Navio (Navy Lieutenant) Fabricio Coloccini are figments of our overzealous imaginations, although the basis of this story is true and something like it did happen during the Falklands War. However, we were aware that if we wrote about soldiers and sailors who were involved and are still alive then the story might easily cause some offence, which is not our intention. Bearing that in mind, we created the 'Nobby' and 'Fabricio' characters to fit in with the story about the sinking of the 'Santé Fe' submarine in 1982.

The Argentinian Republic Armada (ARA) ship 'Santé Fe' was an Argentine submarine that had a bit of history. Commissioned in 1944 she served with the United States Navy under the name USS Catfish and saw action in the Pacific against the forces of Japan in the latter stages of World War Two, she also served with the US Navy during the Korean War. In 1971 she was commissioned into the Argentine Navy and was renamed the 'Santé Fe.' By that time she was outdated and obsolete, but nevertheless supported the Argentine invasion of the Falkland Islands in 1982. On completion of the invasion, the crew of the 'Santé Fe' were tasked with ferrying a party of marines and supplies to Grytviken harbour to capture the Island of South Georgia. They were then told to stand by and await the British Task Force which was heading their way.

Ten days later, HMS Antrim, HMS Brilliant, HMS Plymouth, and HMS Endurance were commanded to retake the Island of South Georgia using Royal Marines and soldiers of the Special Boat Squadron (SBS). The submerged 'Santé Fe' was detected by a helicopter from the British Task Force soon after she'd left Grytviken harbour; another British helicopter crippled the submarine with an anti-shipping missile. Despite not being able to re-submerge, she limped back to the wharf at Grytviken harbour, being harried by machine gun fire from several British helicopters along the way. The 'Santé Fe' suffered serious damage and eventually sank alongside the King Edward Point jetty on

South Georgia with only her conning tower visible above the waterline. Her crew and the Argentinian Marines were all taken prisoner. It wasn't until 1985 that the Royal Navy re-floated the sub and towed her out to sea before scuttling the old girl.

Sergeant 'Nobby' Clarke RM

'Nobby' Clarke was born and raised in the East End of London and despite this fact he still went on to support Chelsea Football Club rather than his local Team of West Ham United, 'Nobby' never went along with the crowd, he was his own person. He joined the Royal Marines in 1973 and, tongue in cheek, tells everyone that he breezed through the commando training saying, "It was a piece of piss really." After completing his training he was posted to a Rifle Company in 45 Commando and completed two tours of duty in Northern Ireland. Just before doing a two year tour at Port Stanley in the Falkland Islands he completed the 'Arctic and Mountain Warfare Cadre' qualifying as a Mountain Leader Grade 2.

His posting to Lympstone as an instructor in 1982 was delayed when Argentina decided to invade the Falkland Islands and Nobby set off to the South Atlantic with the rest of the British Task Force.

Teniente De Navio Fabricio Coloccini

Fabricio is the son of an Argentinian Admiral who commanded a flotilla in the Argentine Navy. He was keen to follow in his father's footsteps and in 1971 he was trained at the Escuela Naval Military Academy and commissioned as a Guardiamarina (Midshipman) the following year. For three years he served on surface ships before asking for a transfer to the Argentine Submarine Service where he enjoyed worked alongside the Coast Guard carrying out fishery inspections. There were some fractious moments when he boarded some of the Soviet and Bulgarian trawlers.

Fabricio was eventually promoted to Teniente De Navio (Lieutenant) and in 1982 he set sail on the 'Santé Fe' with an advance party of Argentinian Marines, they were landed on the island to guide in the main invasion force. He envied the men going ashore and wished he could go with them and felt just as 'gung-ho' after dropping the Marines off at Grytviken. The reality of his situation hit hard when the 'Santé Fe' was attacked by the British helicopters, but he didn't panic, giving orders to the men he commanded and tried to remain calm and aloof, he was, after all, an Officer of the Argentinian Navy.

On King Edward Point Jetty, Nobby was guarding Fabricio, who had surrendered, along with the rest of the 'Santé Fe' crew after their submarine was badly damaged and captured. We think the two men would probably have had a conversation something along the following lines:

Nobby: "Fancy a wet, mate?"

Fabricio: "I am no 'mate' of yours, English! And may I remind you that I am a commissioned officer!'

Nobby: "I couldn't really give a flying fart what you are, mate. To me you're just another prisoner! I'm guarding you – and I'm doing the decent thing by offering you a cup of hot char! Here – take it or leave it!"

Nobby passed a mug of tea to the Argentine Officer.

Fabricio: "Look, er Clarke, you must forgive me. I am unused to being a prisoner of war. There is much for me to learn. I am truly grateful for the hot tea. Thank you"

Nobby: "That's more like it, sir! Come and sit down. Here, you can have one of my biscuits as well."

Fabricio: "Thank you. Chocolate half-coated. Your Royal Navy does rather well for rations."

Nobby: "Two things to note sir, one, these ain't Royal Navy scran, my misses give me a couple of packets just before we shipped out, and two, it ain't my Royal Navy. I'm a Royal Marine and we are nothing to do with the bloody Royal Navy."

Fabricio: "You are a lucky man. I haven't seen my family for quite some time."

Nobby: "It's the life we lead, innit. One minute I'm at home knocking seven bells out of the kids, the next – I'm out here knocking seven bells out of you buggers!"

Fabricio: "I see from your jacket that your name is Clarke. May I know your first name?"

Nobby: "If I told you that sir, I'd have to kill you!"

Fabricio, believing him, is astounded.

Fabricio: "Really! My God! Your rules are so strict?"

Nobby: "Ner, I'm only pulling your leg, boss!"

Fabricio: "Pulling my leg? What does that mean?"
Nobby: "Bloody hell! I'm just having a little joke with you. Everybody knows me as Nobby, Nobby Clarke."

Fabricio: "May I call you Nobby?"

Nobby: "Course you can, sir, but if any of my Officers are around, better not. Don't want to be accused of fraternising, eh."

Fabricio: "I understand. No familiarity. So what is your rank, Nobby?"

Nobby: "Now then sir, don't be a naughty officer. I can't be answering too many questions or I'll get me arse smacked!"

Fabricio: "Of course, forgive me. We must all – how you say – 'Play the Game."

Nobby looks at his watch.

Nobby: "S'Right. Tell you what, boss, I'm bleedin Hank Marvin!"

Fabricio: "Er, Hank Marvin?"

Nobby: "Starvin! I've got are these corned beef sandwiches if you fancy risking one. I'd commit murder for a full English!"

Fabricio: "A full English?"

Nobby: "Yerst – Heinz Beans, Bacon, Fried Bread, Mushrooms, Eggs. That sort of stuff. Put's hairs on yer chest, don't it."

Fabricio: "Do your English ladies eat a "Full English?"

Nobby: "Course they do!"

Fabricio: "Does it put hairs on their chests?"

Nobby: "On my sort of chick it does!"

They both laugh and start to eat the corned beef sandwiches.

Nobby: "'Hairs on their chests.' It's just a figure of speech, innit! These corned beef sarnies are shite! Must've been a bloody ancient cow, it's as tough as old boots!"

Fabricio: "Nothing wrong with the corned beef – it's probably from Argentina!"

Nobby: "Probably is. Funny that innit..."

Fabricio: "What is – funny, Nobby?"

Nobby: Well here we are, officially enemies, knocking seven bells out of each other - you wallop us, we wallop you, we sink your Sub and all that – and here we are scoffing your corned beef. Bleedin' madness."

Fabricio: "Yes, it's a strange world, Nobby."

Nobby: "What's it all about hey, boss?"

Fabricio: "The Malvinas of course."

Nobby: "Naughty Officer – you mean the Falklands!"

He hands a packet of cigarettes to Fabricio.

Nobby: "Ciggie?"

Fabricio: "That is kind of you."

Nobby: "Keep 'em. There's plenty more where they came from."

Nobby lights their cigarettes and they sit there munching on corned beef sandwiches.

Nobby: "So, what is this all about then, boss?"

Fabricio: "As I said, the Malvinas of course. As you well know, the Island belongs to us!"

Nobby: "No it doesn't! You Argies have been very naughty. I'm afraid that you're going to get your arses well and truly kicked and sent back home to lick you wounds."

Fabricio: "We'll see."

Nobby: "Anyway, let's not get into that just now. We'll leave that sort of things to the Admirals and Generals, eh."

Fabricio: Huh, my Father is an Almirante, an Admiral. I have brought shame on him and on my family by surrendering."

Nobby: "No you haven't, sir. It's fortunes of war that's all. Somebody's got to lose – and it's going to be you lot of course. You shouldn't tamper with the Brits. This is just the beginning of the end, innit?"

Fabricio: "What will happen to my submarine?"

Nobby: "Well, it's bollocksed. Pile of bloody scrap metal."

Fabricio: "What will happen to me and my crew?"

Nobby: "I shouldn't worry about that, sir. You'll be treated properly, that's the way we Brits do things. You and your lads will just have to behave and be patient, that's all."

Fabricio: "And then what?"

Nobby: "You'll all get sent back home in one piece, eventually. As I said, we Brits play by the rules."

Fabricio: "I should get back to my crew. Thank you for the tea, sandwich and cigarettes, Nobby. I hope that we meet again under happier circumstances."

Nobby: "Yes, well the next time you're passing Portsmouth, call in and we'll nip out for a pie and a pint. I know a few good pubs."

They both laugh and shake hands.

Fabricio: "I may well take you up on that."

An armed Royal Marine guard arrives and shouts at the Officer.

Guard: "Come on you spick dick-head! Shift your arse!"

Nobby: "Oy you! That's a commissioned officer you're addressing!"
Guard: "Sorry Sergeant. If you'd care to follow me, sir."

Nobby: "And don't be bloody cheeky lad – that could easily be you! Now be nice or I'll insert my boot up your rectum!"

Guard: "Sorry Sergeant."
Nobby: "Show a bit of respect my son."

20. EPILOGUE

Well, dear reader, there you have it, the actual words that we have dreamt up could have been spoken by those in positions of importance at various stages throughout world history. As mentioned in the Preface, no-one really knows exactly what was said during these iconic meetings, we can only presume and fill in the gaps for ourselves because the written word can be somewhat unreliable. A lot of conversations took place behind closed doors without any witnesses and, naturally, are now dimmed by either the passage of time or outright embellishment. So bearing that in mind, what we've written in this book has been done so in a light hearted manner, we sincerely hope that we haven't offended anyone, because that definitely wasn't our intention. Nor did we intend to make light of military violence or the Servicemen and Servicewomen who bravely took up arms, and who continue to do so, in order to defend our country's freedom and beliefs. Both authors have experienced the ugly results of what happens during and after violence has erupted and the distressing fallout that can and is left behind as a result.

One thing about Servicemen and Servicewomen though, especially those who have served in the British Army, Royal Navy, Royal Marines and the Royal Air Force, is that they can usually face dangerous situations and laugh about them afterwards, without making light of what happened. It is their way of coping with the fear and some of the horrific images that they witnessed. Recent conflicts in Iraq and Afghanistan, as in previous wars, have left members of the Armed Forces, on both sides of the divide, with severe mental and physical disabilities which is extremely sad. Conversely, you only have to look at the positive mental attitude of those like Corporal Ricky Fergusson (4th Battalion The Rifles Regiment) after he had suffered the most appalling injuries in Afghanistan. He lost both of his legs, an eye and some of the fingers on both of his hands after setting off an Improvised Explosive Device (IED) when leaving a civilian compound in the Sangin District of Afghanistan. Ricky was awarded an MC (Military Cross) for saving several lives and is just one of many who face up to their disabilities with unquestionable bravery and fortitude. We are grateful to all of them for what they did and are still doing for us, we salute their unquestionable heroism and bravery.

Harry was a
Crap Hat

A Soldier's Story

BRIAN CLACY

TWO MEDICS, ONE NURSE AND A GOB DOCTOR

Two wars in Iraq without fighting

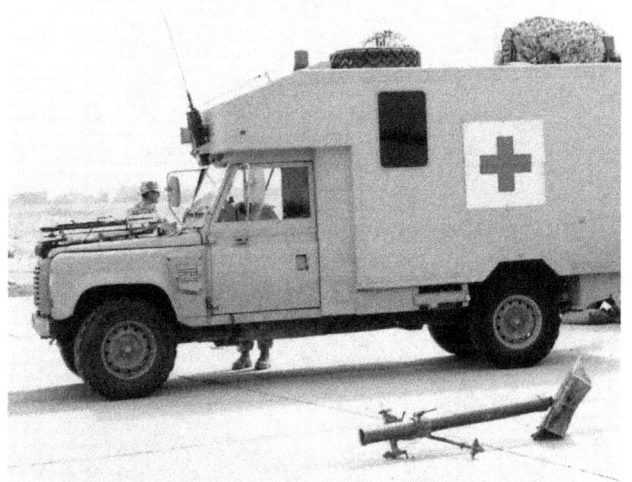

Brian (Harry) Clacy

always
HARRY ^ WAS
A CRAP HAT

Brian (Harry) Clacy

RICKSHAWS, CAMELS AND TAXIS

Rogues, Ruffians and Officers of the
Royal Corps of Transport

Written by **Brian (Harry) Clacy**

CPSIA information can be obtained
at www.ICGtesting.com
Printed in the USA
LVHW041606210819
628458LV00011B/938